In memory of the sweetest perfume, my father
Ilhan Mehmed Lautliev (1925–2007).

Purple Citrus & Sweet Perfume

Cuisine of the Eastern Mediterranean

Silvena Rowe

With a foreword by Heston Blumenthal

Photographs by Jonathan Lovekin

HUTCHINSON

LONDON

Published by Hutchinson 2010

10 9 8 7 6 5 4 3 2

Copyright © Silvena Rowe 2010

Photographs © Jonathan Lovekin

First published in Great Britain in 2010 by Hutchinson

Random House, 20 Vauxhall Bridge Road, London SW1V 2SA

www.rbooks.co.uk

Addresses for companies within The Random House Group Limited can be found at:
www.randomhouse.co.uk/offices.htm

The Random House Group Limited Reg. No. 954009

A CIP catalogue record for this book
is available from the British Library

ISBN 9780091930967

Commissioning Editor: Emma Rose
Managing Editor: Joanna Taylor
Designer: Richard Marston
Cover designer: Greg Heinimann
Stylist: Elif Gönensay – www.elifgonensay.com
Copy-editor: Annie Lee
Cookery assistant: Kerem Delibalta

The Random House Group Limited supports The Forest Stewardship Council (FSC),
the leading international forest certification organisation. All our titles that are printed
on Greenpeace approved FSC certified paper carry the FSC logo. Our paper procurement
policy can be found at www.rbooks.co.uk/environment

Printed and bound by Firmengruppe APPL, aprinta druck, Wemding, Germany

Contents

Foreword by Heston Blumenthal

When Silvena asked me to write a foreword to her book, I couldn't help but say yes. Everything she does, be it writing, broadcasting or cooking, she approaches with the same boundless energy and enthusiasm and her infectious passion is impossible to resist. She has written books and columns, presented television shows, been a consultant to top restaurants and cooked for an impressive line-up of celebrities, and each project is connected by her individual brand of dedication and her original take on food.

As a chef, I find other people's food memories fascinating, and *Purple Citrus & Sweet Perfume* is full of stories and reminiscences that set it apart from most cookbooks. Silvena's nostalgia for the aromas and flavours of her childhood really brings the recipes alive and the book gives us a very personal glimpse at the relatively unexplored food cultures of these Eastern Mediterranean countries.

Her Eastern European heritage gives Silvena a unique perspective on this part of the world, particularly through her father and paternal grandmother who were of Turkish descent, and it is fitting that she is our guide to the unfamiliar dishes, exotic spices and new ingredients of these cuisines.

As well as the food of her childhood, there are more recent discoveries from the restaurants of Damascus and the cafés of Istanbul, and more traditional dishes from the kitchens of the Ottoman Empire. In fact, this stunning book is part travelogue, part memoir, part history lesson and part cookbook. It is beautifully written with a rich mix of evocative stories, poetry, fairy tales and history, woven into the carefully crafted recipes, and the fantastic photographs add to the seductive atmosphere captured by the words. Furthermore, the pages are so packed with Silvena's characteristic enthusiasm and irresistible passion, I defy anyone to resist.

Introduction

In the early part of the twentieth century, when the latest medical breakthroughs were finding their way into the back streets of old Damascus, an elderly blind woman underwent a cataract operation, and afterwards, when she was recovering and the bandages were removed from her eyes, she was asked by the doctor what it was that she could see. 'I can see your face,' she replied.

These plain and simple words serve to underline what I hope to achieve with this book. To open your eyes to the cuisines of the Eastern Mediterranean, to allow you to see and taste for yourself the wonderful panorama of fruits, vegetables, meat and rice dishes that this region has to offer; to wander through the kitchens of Turkey, Syria, Jordan and Lebanon, the cuisines of Europeans and Arabs, of Muslims, Christians and Jews, discovering as we go the old world of the Ottoman Empire.

For 500 years the Ottomans ruled what is modern-day Bulgaria – where I grew up – leaving only in the latter part of the nineteenth century. What followed was, in culinary terms, a black hole.

At the very zenith of their power the Ottomans controlled not just the Eastern Mediterranean, but most of the Balkans, much of the Caucasus, the Crimea and the Middle East. The cities of Athens, Budapest, Belgrade, Sarajevo, Bucharest, Sofia, Beirut, Damascus, Baghdad, Jerusalem, Mecca, Cairo, Alexandria, Tunis, everything to the very gates of Vienna, fell under the Sultan's power.

The Ottomans were no stick-in-the-muds – as their armies rolled through the neighbouring countries they embraced the local cultures and, more importantly for this book, the local cuisines. The vast tracts of land over which they held sway offered unmatched fertility, and, just as the sun never set on the British Empire, so it is said that the fruits and vegetables of all seasons could be found in the markets of Constantinople (the Ottoman capital and now modern-day Istanbul), such was their all-encompassing power.

The entire region became a melting pot of cuisines, bringing a melange of tastes, colours and smells. Chefs were invited (or enslaved) from across the Empire and beyond, and Armenian, Greek, Persian, Egyptian, Serbian, Hungarian and even French chefs came to Constantinople, first to the Sultan's Topkapi Palace, then to the homes of the fabulously wealthy. Even the Spice Road, the most important factor in culinary history, was under the Sultan's control. So only the best ingredients were allowed to be traded under the strict standards established by the courts, which meant recipes of unparalleled flavour could be produced. Consequently, a grand gastronomic tradition was

developed by the aristocratic elite of the city, a culture that covered everything – the ingredients, the methods of cooking, the kinds of food, the kitchens and even the table manners – and spread to the furthest regions of the Empire.

In its heyday the wealth and splendour of the Topkapi Palace were renowned across the world. The gardens, courtyards and vistas, the glittering domes and minarets, the baths and marble fountains, the carpets, textiles and ceramics, the paintings, the jewels, the objets d'art. The swords, the hair plucked from the beard of the prophet, the holy mantle and other relics of Muhammad brought from Mecca, the Meissen and Limoges porcelain presented by European royalty, the great fireplaces, the thrones, the Iznik tiles in all their brilliant colours. The sea-view windows encased with mother-of-pearl shutters.

The Ottomans, open to all the sensory delights, were absolutely crazy about haute cuisine, and the vastness of their kitchens almost defies comprehension. Housed under ten domes, at their height the Topkapi kitchens employed 1,300 staff. Hundreds of cooks, specialising in different categories of dishes – soups, pilafs, kebabs, vegetables, fish, breads, pastries, sweets, helva, syrups, jams and beverages – fed, on feast days and special celebrations, as many as 10,000 people a day. The Sultan had his own personal staff of seventeen speciality chefs and still more for his family. His food was prepared with great ceremony, and never consisted of fewer than twenty separate dishes. Each dish was brought in one at a time, covered and sealed with a ribbon to prevent it from being poisoned.

Following the example of the Palace, all the grand Ottoman houses boasted elaborate kitchens and competed in preparing feasts for each other as well as for the general public. In fact, in each neighbourhood at least one household would open its doors to anyone who happened to stop by for dinner during the holy month of Ramadan, or during other festive occasions. So it was that the cuisine evolved and spread, even to the most modest corners of the Eastern Mediterranean.

It would be impossible to cover every cuisine deriving from the Ottoman Empire, so I have stuck, with the odd sidetrack, to the eastern end of the Mediterranean. Here you will find a modern twist on the classic recipes of this rich culinary tradition, following in the footsteps of the great Ottoman chefs who combined the sweet and the sour, the fresh and the dried, honey and cinnamon, saffron and sumac, scented rose and orange flower waters with the most magical of spices. This book is proof, if proof were needed, that there is a lot more to the Mediterranean than just Italy and France.

Chef's Note

All **herbs** listed in the ingredients are dried and ground, unless otherwise stated. When I refer to a large bunch of fresh herbs this is a rough guide to what you'll be able to find in your greengrocer's – when using fresh herbs, most of the time you can use as much as you wish to bring the flavour out. When a smaller quantity is required for a more subtle flavour I've indicated that you use a 50g pack instead, which I find is the standard size available in supermarkets.

When it comes to **olive oil**, I always use the best-quality extra virgin oil I can find, as this will always have the most satisfying flavour. But it's fine to use whatever olive oil you have to hand. I also often recommend cooking with clarified butter (ghee) as it doesn't burn as easily or turn brown.

I **season** a lot of my dishes with freshly ground sea salt and black pepper. Always use as little or as much as suits your tastes.

At the end of the book you'll find a useful list of **store-cupboard essentials** appropriate to the recipes in this book. It includes the simple recipes for two classic Eastern Mediterranean spice mixes that I often use – za'atar and baharat – which are both also available to buy ready-mixed (the Bart's spices brand does both these blends, as well as the more obscure spices and herbs such as sumac and chervil). It also features easy instructions for making pomegranate molasses, another Eastern Mediterranean staple.

Finally, **cooking times** are shown in degrees centigrade for fan-assisted ovens and gas mark. For non-fan-assisted ovens add 20 degrees to the temperature indicated.

Hakawati Abu Shadi

Early one morning I left the centre of Damascus and travelled east, thirty kilometres out through the suburbs where the remnants of olive, lemon, pomegranate and orange groves and ancient farmhouses can still be glimpsed. As we neared our goal, the home of Abu Shadi, the apricot, the cherry and apple orchards asserted themselves. Even for my driver, a resident of the old city, this was an adventure, and I asked him if he knew of the Hakawati.

'Where I live,' the driver replied, 'everyone is a Hakawati, everyone tells stories, and we do not need books.' A Hakawati is a storyteller, and Abu Shadi is the last Hakawati in Damascus – some believe that he is the last Hakawati in the whole of Syria. There is no greater tradition in Syria than that of storytelling.

Abu Shadi was born and raised in the centre of the old town. From eight years old, he would go with his father to the Al-Nafurah Café, next to the grand mosque, and listen, fascinated, as the Hakawati of the time told his tales. Every day he would go, and when the Hakawati finished, Abu would beg to be given the Hakawati's book to look at. When Abu was twelve years old his father died, but as the café owner was a close family friend, he was still welcomed and became like a son to the café owner.

The last of the old Hakawatis passed away in the seventies and Abu Shadi was asked if he would take on the mantle at the Al-Nafurah. He was unsure, times had changed, there was a television in every home, competition to the old ways. But the café owner was persistent, insisting the people still wanted a Hakawati, and in particular they wanted Abu Shadi. Only he knew the language in which the stories must be told, the style, the content. Finally he agreed.

'As I sat on the Hakawati chair the café was full, the sweet smell of apple-flavoured hookah tobacco in the air, the expectant faces of the patrons,' Abu recalled. 'I was trembling, my heart beating fast, I wanted to run, but all were looking at me, strong eyes that encouraged me to begin the tales.'

At first Abu believed that his style was too wooden, his narrating skills but a poor imitation of those Hakawatis that had gone before. Not long after he began, a famous Lebanese actress came to the café to listen to him. Afterwards they were introduced and Abu decided to ask her advice. She told him that if she had a stick, she would beat him with it. He was astonished and asked her why. She told him that he was merely repeating the words, he did not look the people in the eye, did not convey the passion of the story. So she took the book and she showed him how to act and use his body language. Abu told me he would have been nothing without her help. She invited him to Beirut and showed him how to use the tone of his voice, to move his body, his hands, his arms, his legs, each movement to convey meaning and emotion. These were the most important lessons he ever learned.

As we sat in the garden of Abu Shadi's home, he told me the beginning of a tale, that of Prince Antar and the beautiful Abla, her 'face like the moon, lips like peanuts, nose like a noodle, cheeks like Syrian apples, eyes like a gazelle, hair like a long strand of silk'. This was Abu's first story as a Hakawati, and he returned night after night to tell it at the Al-Nafurah. For the hour between prayers, he would enthusiastically embellish, bang his flat sword in his hand, switch from voice to voice, and repeat key phrases in several languages so that all his audience would understand.

Much as I would like to include the tales that Abu Shadi tells, they would be far too long, for they are tales of truly epic proportion, stories of a great people renowned for their chivalry, truthfulness and generosity. Tales that can quite literally take a year in the telling, as they're entwined with anecdotes, comments and adaptation for modern times. But they never lose sight of from whence they came. Likewise I have done just so with these recipes, adapting and changing a classic cuisine for modern times and modern ingredients, just as the Ottomans themselves moved with the ever-changing tides.

MEZZE

In the time of Sultan Selim, there lived in Constantinople a drunkard, perhaps the only one in the whole of Turkey, and as a consequence his behaviour was discussed in both high and low society.

The Sultan, hearing of this man, called him to the palace and demanded to know why he disobeyed the prophet.

The drunkard replied that alcohol was a benefit to man, that it made the deaf hear, the blind see, the lame walk and the poor rich.

The Sultan, wishing to find the truth of the matter, sent his servants to find four men so afflicted; thus found, they were brought to the palace and each was served raki. Before long, the deaf man announced, 'I can hear the sound of great rumbling!' The blind man replied, 'I can see him; it is an enemy that seeks our destruction!' The lame man said, 'Show him to me and I will despatch him!' and the poor man said, 'Do not be afraid to kill him, for I have his blood money in my pocket.'

As these things were being said a funeral happened to pass the palace. The drunkard called from the window for it to be halted, rushed outside and opened the lid of the coffin. He spoke to the dead man and leaned down to hear his reply. Then the funeral went on its way.

'What did you ask the dead man?' asked the Sultan. 'And what did he say?'

'I asked him where he was going, and of what did he die. He told me that he was going to paradise and that he had died of drinking raki without a mezze.'

Adapted from *Told in the Coffee House*, stories collected in Istanbul by Cyrus Adler and Allan Ramsay (1898)

Mezze

Mezze is about spending time together, enjoying long warm evenings with family and friends, sharing anecdotes and stories of life over a leisurely meal. The Eastern Mediterranean mezze brings together a glittering array of dishes: rustic bean and mustard green salads, velvety tahini-based hummus and smooth vegetable purées, crunchy falafels and the wonderful flavours of crimson beetroot and emerald-green spinach. Not to mention the sophisticated sumac- and za'atar-flavoured seafood and delicately baked pastries accompanying pomegranate and walnut salads enriched with nigella and sesame seeds, all topped off with the cooling texture of natural yoghurt. The list is endless, but it is not just about the food as nourishment and satisfying your belly; it is about the colours, the textures, the combinations – a true feast for the eyes.

Mezze is in general an extremely healthy way of eating, combining as it does the most simple and basic of fresh ingredients, making it perfect for the twenty-first-century stomach. So enjoy it for breakfast, as a snack, for lunch or for dinner. To my mind there can be no particular order to a mezze – hot can be eaten with warm, vegetable with meat dishes, it is whatever you want it to be. My personal preference would be something like this: a combination of veggie-based tzatzikis, veggie-based hummus, then falafels, seasonal herb salads topped with white cheeses, followed by stuffed vine leaves, kofte, and finally okra cooked with fresh tomatoes, and a crispy börek.

Suzme Rolled in Za'atar, Sumac and Pistachios

Suzme is strained yoghurt, known in the Middle East as labne. When yoghurt is strained, and the mixture drains away, it becomes very thick. Left for twenty-four hours, it takes on the texture of cream cheese, thereby allowing it to be rolled in a variety of coatings, such as herbs, nuts and seeds. For this recipe you will need to use a good-quality, full-fat, plain yoghurt without additives.

Za'atar is a typical Middle Eastern blend of herbs and spices. It is available ready-mixed at most Middle Eastern and Turkish shops, and Waitrose stock a blend of it made by Bart's, but it is also very easy to make at home. A recipe for making it is included on p. 250.

800g full-fat plain yoghurt

200g goat's cheese

80g pistachios,
½ finely chopped,
½ finely ground

2 tablespoons za'atar
(see p. 250 for the recipe)

2 tablespoons crushed or ground sumac

2 pieces of muslin or cheesecloth approximately 30 × 30cm

1 or 2 days in advance

Place the yoghurt in the centre of the double-layered muslin or cheesecloth. Standing over a sink, twist the muslin around the yoghurt until you have a tight ball. Tie the top with some string and suspend the ball (I tie it to the tap) for a day or so. You will end up with yoghurt of a very thick consistency, which is known in the Eastern Mediterranean as suzme. It will be roughly half the weight that you started with.

On the day

Place the suzme in a bowl with the goat's cheese and combine until smooth. Put aside a small quantity of the chopped and ground pistachios.

Shape the mixture into quenelles, using roughly a teaspoonful at a time. Roll a third of the quenelles in the za'atar, coating each one generously, and put to one side. Repeat this with the remaining quenelles, rolling half in the sumac and the other half in the pistachios. When making the pistachio quenelles, for variety of texture, you can do some with just the ground pistachios, some with just the chopped pistachios and some with both.

Arrange all the quenelles on a platter, sprinkle with the remaining pistachios, season and serve with wild greens and warm bread.

SERVES 8

Crispy Spiced King Prawns
with Avocado and Tahini Sauce

- 1 **large ripe avocado, peeled and stone removed**
- 1 **garlic clove, crushed**
- 2 **tablespoons olive oil**
- 1 **tablespoon tahini**
- 3 **tablespoons lemon juice**

zest of 1 **lemon**

- 1 **tablespoon plain flour**
- 1 **tablespoon semolina**
- ½ **teaspoon ground cumin**
- ½ **teaspoon crushed or ground sumac**
- ½ **teaspoon ground ginger**
- ½ **teaspoon ground coriander**
- 1 **tablespoon black sesame seeds**
- 300g **king prawns, shelled and heads removed**
- 4 **tablespoons olive oil**

To make the sauce

Combine all the ingredients in a food processor and pulse to purée.

To cook the prawns

Combine the flour, semolina, cumin, sumac, ginger, coriander and sesame seeds in a bowl, then season. In a separate bowl, cover the shelled prawns with 2 tablespoons of the olive oil.

Heat the remaining olive oil in a non-stick pan. Dip each prawn in the flour and spice mixture, coating them well. Sauté the prawns for 2–4 minutes in the pan, a few at a time, until golden brown.

Season the sauce and serve with the crispy prawns.

SERVES 4

Haydari – Yoghurt and Feta Dip

Haydari is a thick and voluptuously creamy dip made with strained yoghurt or suzme. This is something that I vividly remember from my childhood, forming part of a wonderful breakfast served with freshly baked bread. My mother made her haydari with home-made yoghurt, adding chopped olives and a hint of olive oil, but my favourite version is this one, using feta cheese and sweet paprika. Make your own yoghurt if you've got the time, but otherwise shop-bought thick yoghurt works almost as well.

100g **feta, crumbled**

300ml **suzme (strained yoghurt, see instructions on p. 22)**

2 **garlic cloves, crushed**

leaves of 6 **fresh mint sprigs, finely chopped**

2 **tablespoons walnuts, finely chopped**

½ **teaspoon sweet paprika**

1 **tablespoon olive oil**

Place the feta in a bowl and mash with a fork. Add the suzme, garlic and mint, and combine well. Season with black pepper.

Serve sprinkled with the walnuts and sweet paprika, and drizzled with olive oil.

SERVES 6

Tahini, Lemon and Sumac Sauce

1–2 **tablespoons water**

3 **tablespoons tahini paste**

1 **teaspoon ground cumin**

juice of 2 **small lemons**

2 **garlic cloves, crushed**

½ **teaspoon crushed or ground sumac**

2 **tablespoons olive oil**

1 **teaspoon black sesame seeds**

Mix the tahini, cumin and the lemon juice in a bowl. Slowly stir in the water, a little at a time, until you have a consistency that resembles double cream. Then add the garlic, and season.

Combine the sumac with the olive oil and drizzle over the sauce. Sprinkle with sesame seeds and serve.

SERVES 6–8

Stuffed Vine Leaves with Summer Squash, Rice and Pine Nuts

FOR THE VINE LEAVES

50	vine leaves, fresh or preserved, or a 300g packet of vine leaves

FOR THE STUFFING

4	tablespoons olive oil
1	large onion, finely chopped
500g	summer squash, peeled, seeds removed, finely cubed
90g	short-grain rice
8	fresh oregano sprigs, finely chopped
8	fresh tarragon sprigs, finely chopped
50g	toasted pine nuts, roughly chopped

TO SERVE

200ml	yoghurt
	zest and juice of ½ lemon
1	tablespoon olive oil

To prepare the vine leaves

If you can't find fresh vine leaves then use preserved, and make sure that they are washed and drained well. Select 40 good leaves, and put the rest to one side. Boil a saucepan of water, remove from the heat and drop in the vine leaves to blanch. After 5 minutes, remove the leaves and pat dry with a thick paper towel.

To make the stuffing

Heat the olive oil in a deep pan over a medium heat and sauté the onion for 3 minutes until just translucent. Add the summer squash and cook for 5 minutes. Add the rice, combining it well with the other ingredients, then stir in the oregano, tarragon and pine nuts, and season. Continue to cook for 10 minutes.

To make the parcels

Lay out a cooled, blanched leaf, shiny side down, and place a small amount of the summer squash mixture in the centre – just enough to still be able to comfortably wrap the leaf around the mixture. Fold the bottom edge nearest you over the filling, then fold in the two sides and tightly roll away from you into a neat parcel.

To cook the vine leaves

Line the bottom of a medium-sized saucepan with 4 or 5 of the unblanched leaves that you put aside. Arrange the stuffed vine leaves, seam side down, in the prepared saucepan, keeping them nice and tight in layers. Arrange the remaining unblanched leaves on top of the stuffed parcels. Add just enough water to cover. Weigh the parcels down with a plate to keep them in place. Simmer on a gentle heat for 45–50 minutes.

To serve

Combine the yoghurt, lemon and olive oil, and season. Serve the stuffed vine leaves warm or cold, accompanied by the lemon and yoghurt sauce.

MAKES 40

Aubergine, Aleppo Chilli and Pomegranate Jam

This chilli jam is wonderful as an accompaniment to any meat dish, or just spread on bread and eaten on its own. Aleppo chilli is mild, sweet, fruity and slightly smoky. You might have to look around for it, but it is available in many Turkish and Middle Eastern food stores, in red and green variations, and you buy it dried. If you have trouble finding it, substitute mild red chilli flakes and a teaspoon of smoked paprika.

The city of Aleppo is in northern Syria, and is claimed to be one of the oldest inhabited cities in the world, having been founded more than 3,000 years ago.

1	large aubergine
3	tablespoons olive oil
1	teaspoon dried Aleppo chilli, finely chopped
1	garlic clove, crushed
½	teaspoon ground coriander
½	teaspoon ground allspice
2	ripe tomatoes, finely chopped
2	teaspoons pomegranate molasses (see p. 249 for the recipe)
seeds from 1	small pomegranate
50g	pack of fresh coriander, finely chopped
zest of ½	lemon

Wash and trim the aubergine, then slice thinly.

Heat the olive oil in a heavy non-stick saucepan and add the aubergine slices a few at a time, cooking them until golden brown. Stir in the Aleppo chilli, garlic, coriander and allspice. Don't worry if the aubergine slices break up. Add the chopped tomatoes and pomegranate molasses and simmer on a low heat until the liquid is almost gone and the aubergine is soft and mushy. Transfer to a bowl and allow to cool.

Add the pomegranate seeds and fresh coriander to the cooled mixture, combine, and season to taste. Sprinkle with the lemon zest before serving.

SERVES 6

Syrian Za'atar Bread with Thyme Flowers

Breads are an essential part of the mezze table. Traditional breads, especially flat breads, were baked in a clay oven known as a taboon, *where a disc of dough would be stuck against the oven wall and within 1–2 minutes it would become deliciously crisp on the outside and velvety and soft on the inside. Za'atar bread is exactly that, a flat bread, not that dissimilar to pitta, but flavoured with za'atar – a blend of herbs and spices.*

FOR THE DOUGH

175ml	**warm water**
3	**teaspoons dry active yeast**
600g	**plain flour**
300g	**wholewheat flour**
275ml	**warm milk**
2	**tablespoons za'atar** (see p. 250 for the recipe)
100ml	**olive oil**
1	**teaspoon sea salt**

TO SERVE

2	**tablespoons fresh thyme flowers**

To make the dough

In a bowl, combine the warm water and yeast and allow to stand for 10 minutes, by which time it will be foaming.

Add the warm milk to the yeast mixture. Sift the plain and wholewheat flour into a separate large mixing bowl and make a well in the centre of the flour. Add the yeast mixture to the well and stir to combine. Then, using your hands, knead the mixture into a soft, sticky dough. Shape the dough into a ball, place in a flour-dusted bowl, covered with plastic wrap, and allow to rest for an hour.

Preheat the oven to 240°C fan/gas mark 9.

When the dough has risen, punch it down once with your fist to knock the air out of it. Cut the dough into 16 pieces, rolling each piece into a ball. Using a rolling pin, flatten them into discs, 12cm in diameter. Arrange the discs on baking trays, cover with clingfilm and allow to rise for 20–30 minutes.

Mix the za'atar with the olive oil and drizzle over the risen dough discs. Press the discs down with your thumb and season generously with the sea salt. Bake the dough discs in the oven for 4–5 minutes, until they puff up, keeping a close eye on their progress as the bread can burn very easily.

To serve

Sprinkle with the fresh thyme flowers and serve warm or cold.

MAKES 16

Red Lentil Kofte with Pomegranate and Coriander Salad

This recipe comes from the Zencefil café-restaurant in Istanbul, one of the most popular vegetarian restaurants in the city; it was given to me by my friend and the proprietor, Ferda.

This is easy to prepare and a perfect light snack for summer days. Zencefil serves the little kofte with a simple green salad.

Turkish red pepper paste can be bought from most Turkish and Middle Eastern shops. If you can't get hold of any, use tomato purée instead.

FOR THE KOFTE

- 2 **tablespoons olive oil**
- 1 **large red onion, finely chopped**
- 1 **tablespoon ground cumin**
- 1 **teaspoon paprika**
- 1 **tablespoon za'atar (see p. 250 for the recipe)**
- 100g **red lentils**
- 1 **tablespoon pomegranate molasses (see p. 249 for the recipe)**
- 300ml **water**
- 100g **finely ground bulgur**
- 50g **pack of fresh coriander, finely chopped**
- 1 **tablespoon mild red pepper paste or tomato purée**

FOR THE SALAD

- **seeds from 1 pomegranate**
- 50g **pack of fresh coriander, finely chopped**
- **juice and zest of 1 small lemon**
- 3 **tablespoons olive oil**

To make the kofte

Heat the olive oil in a saucepan and sauté the red onion for 2–3 minutes. Add the cumin, paprika and za'atar, and cook for a further 2 minutes. Stir in the lentils and, lastly, pour in the pomegranate molasses and water. Cover and leave to simmer for 8–10 minutes, until the lentils are almost cooked. Add the bulgur, combine well and season. Tip the mixture into a bowl and allow to cool.

Once cool, stir in the coriander and red pepper paste. Cover and refrigerate for 30 minutes to set.

To make the salad

Combine all the ingredients in a bowl.

To serve

Shape the kofte mixture into mini balls and make a small indentation in the centre of each. Spoon in the pomegranate and coriander salad.

MAKES 30

White Butter Bean, Feta and Za'atar Crush

Fifty kilometres west of Damascus in Syria, perched 1,500 metres up the side of the Kalamun Mountains near the entrance to a gorge, lies the ancient village of Ma'alula. In fact the name of the village means exactly that, 'The Entrance'.

The Syrians strive to keep its unique character. So, quite rightly, cars are banned from its streets. After the long, hot and dusty ride from the Syrian capital, my head filled with the Hakawati's stories, we trudged wearily up a hill and staggered into a promising-looking café. I had visions of a bustling eatery, filled with locals tucking into some delicacy or other, imbibing cooling drinks made with lemons, or maybe yoghurt with crushed ice.

The Al-Barakeh café sadly failed my aesthetic visions and the tables were empty of customers. We were greeted by the café owner who immediately offered us something to drink on the house – that's Syrian hospitality for you! I naturally felt obliged to order some food and more drinks, but an empty café does not inspire confidence and I must confess to wondering out loud what he might be able to offer.

Even in the tourist season, the owner explained, things were difficult, and this being October, there was little business. But he smiled one of those enigmatic smiles that Syrians seem to use for almost any occasion, and said that he would do his best.

It was this simple but wonderful dish, made with local goat's cheese and served with freshly baked flat bread, that he brought to the table.

200g	**dried butter beans, soaked overnight with the skins removed**
1	**large garlic bulb**
6	**tablespoons olive oil**
juice of ½	**small lemon**
zest of 1	**lemon**
½	**large bunch of fresh mint, leaves only, finely chopped**
½	**teaspoon cumin seeds, toasted and ground**
150g	**feta, crumbled**
1	**teaspoon za'atar (see p. 250 for the recipe)**

Preheat the oven to 200°C fan/gas mark 7.

Bring a saucepan of water to boil and add the pre-soaked, skinned beans. Reduce to a simmer and cook for 30 minutes until the beans are soft and mushy, then season. Allow to cool, then process to a rough purée.

Meanwhile, place the garlic on a small baking tray, drizzle with a little olive oil and roast in the oven for 30 minutes. Cool, then squeeze the garlic out of its skin and add to the mashed beans. Stir half the olive oil into the bean and garlic mixture. Mix in the lemon juice and zest. Then add the mint, cumin and feta, stirring until you have a rough chunky purée, and season.

Place in a serving dish, drizzle with the rest of the olive oil and sprinkle with the za'atar. Serve with flat bread.

SERVES 8

There was once a man called Hussein who saved up his money so that he might pilgrimage to Mecca. When the time came, he had more money than was required to make the journey. He thought that he might give the excess to the poor, but what if he needed it upon his return?

After much deliberation he decided to leave the money with his neighbour, but not trusting him, he put the money in a bag and placed it in a jar, then filled the jar with oil and olives. Hussein went to the neighbour and asked him if he would look after the jar of olives while he travelled to Mecca, to which he agreed.

It so happened that while Hussein was away, his neighbour received some guests, and as was his way, he offered them raki, but was ashamed that he had no mezze to offer. Knowing that the olives would be easy to replace, he opened the jar, and there, at the bottom, he found the money in a bag. The neighbour was completely mystified, but put the coins in his pocket.

When Hussein returned from Mecca, he went to the neighbour and retrieved the olive jar, and to his horror, found that the money was gone! He angrily demanded to know where the money had gone.

'I can only but think,' the neighbour said innocently, 'that the coins have turned into olives.'

That night, Hussein, a patient man, thought of a plan to get his money back.

From that day on, Hussein sought out his neighbour's company and they became even firmer friends than they had been before, and the son of Hussein became a friend of his neighbour's son.

Hussein purchased a monkey and kept it in a cage. He had also made an effigy of his neighbour, and the effigy was placed opposite the cage. Twice a day, for many months, food for the monkey was placed on the effigy of the neighbour, and Hussein would open the cage saying, 'Go to your father,' and the monkey would sit on the effigy's shoulder and eat his food.

One day, the neighbour's son was asked to Hussein's house so that he might play, and while he was there, he was invited to stay for a few days.

The neighbour came that evening to find out why his son had not returned, only to be told by Hussein that his son had changed into a monkey, and that becoming angry the monkey had had to be locked in a cage!

Hussein showed his neighbour the monkey, and upon seeing the neighbour, and recognising him as the effigy, the monkey screamed for his food.

The next day the neighbour dragged Hussein before the courts to explain himself. Hussein brought the monkey along so that, God willing, they would see that he spoke the truth. The monkey was brought in and the cage opened. Hussein said, 'Go to your father' and the monkey leapt on to the neighbour's shoulder. The neighbour protested that it was impossible for a child to be changed into a monkey, that it was against the laws of nature.

But Hussein stepped forward and declared that this was not true, that his neighbour had witnessed with his own eyes that money could be turned into olives, so why not a boy into a monkey?

Adapted from *Told in the Coffee House*, stories collected
in Istanbul by Cyrus Adler and Allan Ramsay (1898)

Jerusalem Artichoke Hummus Topped with Lamb and Sumac

This is another flavourful dish that I tried at the Al-Barakeh in Ma'alula, prepared along with a classic hummus. This version is made from Jerusalem artichokes instead of chickpeas, making the dish lighter.

FOR THE LAMB

300g	**lamb neck fillet**
2	**teaspoons crushed or ground sumac**
2	**tablespoons olive oil**

FOR THE HUMMUS

500g	**Jerusalem artichokes, peeled and chopped**
2	**tablespoons tahini**
2	**garlic cloves, crushed**
4	**tablespoons lemon juice**
3	**teaspoons cumin seeds, toasted and ground**
6	**tablespoons olive oil**

Preheat the oven to 200°C fan/gas mark 7.

To cook the lamb

Place the lamb fillet in a roasting tray, sprinkle with half the sumac, and season. Rub with 2 tablespoons of olive oil and roast for 25–30 minutes, depending on how pink you like your lamb. Remove from the oven and allow to rest for 10 minutes.

To make the hummus

Place the Jerusalem artichokes in a saucepan and cover with cold water. Bring to the boil and cook on a medium heat for 12–15 minutes until soft. Drain and cool.

Purée the artichokes in a food processor. Add the tahini, garlic, lemon juice and cumin. Switch your machine to pulse and gradually drizzle in the oil, and season.

To serve

Thinly slice the lamb. Spoon the hummus into a serving dish and arrange the lamb slices on top. Then sprinkle with the remaining sumac.

SERVES 4

Lamb and Pistachio Kofte
with Tahini and Pistachio Sauce

FOR THE SAUCE

200g	**shelled unsalted pistachios**
3	**garlic cloves, crushed**
150g	**tahini**
juice of 2	**lemons**
3–4	**tablespoons water**

FOR THE KOFTE

400g	**minced lamb**
1	**onion, grated**
3	**garlic cloves, crushed**
50g	**currants**
50g	**pistachios, roughly chopped**
½	**teaspoon sweet paprika**
¼	**teaspoon ground allspice**
¼	**teaspoon ground cinnamon**
½	**large bunch of fresh mint, finely chopped**
½	**large bunch of fresh parsley, finely chopped**
5–8	**tablespoons olive oil**

To make the sauce

Lightly toast the pistachios by placing them in a dry frying pan and stirring over a medium heat until lightly golden. Allow to cool and put a few aside to use as garnish later. Place the rest in a food processor until finely ground.

In a small bowl combine the garlic, tahini and lemon, and season. Then add 3–4 tablespoons of water so that the paste becomes thinner. Beat until you get the smooth consistency of double cream. Finally, add the ground pistachios and mix in well. Refrigerate until needed.

To make the kofte

Combine all the ingredients except the oil, season, then shape into small golf-ball-sized meatballs. Heat the olive oil in a large non-stick pan. Fry the kofte, a few at a time, for 8–10 minutes, until golden brown and cooked right through.

Serve with the tahini and pistachio sauce.

SERVES 6

Crunchy Red Swiss Chard Falafel

4 tablespoons olive oil

1 red onion, finely chopped

2 teaspoons ground cumin

¼ teaspoon ground allspice

500g red Swiss chard, roughly chopped

220ml milk

100g chickpea flour

3 tablespoons cooked chickpeas

3 tablespoons lemon juice

oil for deep frying

Heat 1 tablespoon of olive oil and sauté the onion, cumin and allspice for 3–4 minutes. Set aside in a bowl.

Fill a large saucepan with water and bring to the boil. Drop in the chard and blanch for 2 minutes. Drain immediately and, once they're cool enough to handle, squeeze the leaves dry.

In a medium non-stick pan, bring the milk to the boil then reduce to a simmer. Little by little, whisk in the chickpea flour until you have a smooth paste. Keep the mixture moving to avoid lumps. Then season, add the remaining olive oil and cook on a low heat for 8 minutes, stirring all the time with a wooden spoon. Like choux pastry, the mixture will come away from the sides of the pan and work into a ball, solidifying as it is heated.

Cool the ball of paste, then mix in the sautéed onions, chickpeas, lemon juice and blanched chard. Using your hands, mould the mixture into small balls and arrange on a tray. Chill in the fridge for a couple of hours.

In a pan, heat until very hot enough oil to cover the falafel balls. Carefully place the falafel into the oil and cook for 3–4 minutes, until golden brown. Remove with a slotted spoon and place on kitchen paper to drain.

Delicious served with tahini, sumac and lemon sauce (see p. 25 for the recipe).

SERVES 6

Crimson Beetroot Falafel

4 tablespoons olive oil

1 large onion, finely chopped

2 teaspoons ground cumin

¼ teaspoon ground allspice

approx. 400g uncooked beetroot

220ml milk

100g chickpea flour

3 tablespoons cooked chickpeas

2 tablespoons lemon juice

vegetable oil for deep frying

Heat 1 tablespoon of olive oil and sauté the onion, cumin and allspice for 3–4 minutes. Set aside in a bowl.

Cook the beetroot in plenty of water until three-quarters cooked (roughly 20 minutes for medium-sized beets). Drain, cool and peel the beetroot and grate on a medium-sized grater (you might want to use rubber gloves to do this!).

In a medium non-stick pan, bring the milk to the boil then reduce to a simmer. Little by little, whisk in the chickpea flour until you have a smooth paste. Keep the mixture moving to avoid lumps. Season, then add the remaining olive oil and cook on a low heat for 8 minutes, stirring all the time with a wooden spoon. Like choux pastry, the mixture will come away from the sides of the pan and work into a ball, solidifying as it is heated.

Cool the ball of paste, then mix in the sautéed onions, chickpeas, lemon juice and grated beetroot. Using your hands, mould the mixture into small balls and arrange on a tray. Chill in the fridge for a couple of hours.

In a pan, heat until very hot enough oil to cover the falafel balls. Carefully place the falafel into the oil and cook for 3–4 minutes, until golden brown. Remove with a slotted spoon and place on kitchen paper to drain.

SERVES 6

Beetroot, Courgette and Spinach Tzatziki

FOR THE BEETROOT TZATZIKI

- 4 **medium beets, roasted and grated**
- 2 **garlic cloves, crushed**
- 3 **tablespoons lemon juice**
- 300ml **suzme (strained yoghurt, see instructions on p. 22)**
- 2–3 **tablespoons olive oil**
- 2 **tablespoons parsley, finely chopped**
- 2 **tablespoons walnuts, roughly chopped**

FOR THE COURGETTE TZATZIKI

- 2–3 **tablespoons olive oil**
- 4 **small courgettes, finely sliced**
- 2 **tablespoons fresh thyme leaves**
- 2 **garlic cloves, crushed**
- 3 **tablespoons lemon juice**
- 300ml **suzme (strained yoghurt, see instructions on p. 22)**
- 2 **tablespoons pine nuts, lightly toasted**

FOR THE SPINACH TZATZIKI

- 2–3 **tablespoons olive oil**
- 2 **garlic cloves, crushed**
- 400g **fresh spinach**
- 3 **tablespoons lemon juice**
- 300ml **suzme (strained yoghurt, see instructions on p. 22)**
- 2 **tablespoons sesame seeds, toasted**

To make the beetroot tzatziki

Combine the grated beetroot, garlic, lemon juice and suzme, and season. Serve drizzled with the olive oil, and sprinkled with the parsley and walnuts.

To make the courgette tzatziki

Heat half the olive oil in a non-stick pan and gently sauté the courgettes and fresh thyme for 5–6 minutes, stirring all the time. Remove from the heat and allow to cool.

Combine the cooled courgette, garlic, lemon juice and suzme, and season. Serve drizzled with the remaining olive oil, and sprinkled with the pine nuts.

To make the spinach tzatziki

Heat the olive oil in a large pan and sauté the garlic, then add the spinach and cook for just a couple of minutes. Drain very well, discarding any liquid. Allow the spinach to cool and squeeze with your hands until as dry as possible.

Combine the cooled spinach, lemon juice and suzme, and season. Serve sprinkled with the sesame seeds.

SERVES 6

Lamb and Spinach Yoghurt Pastry Pyramids

FOR THE PASTRY

400g	self-raising flour
80g	cold butter, cubed
¼	teaspoon salt
1	egg yolk
80ml	yoghurt
2	tablespoons water
1	tablespoon cumin seeds
1	egg yolk, beaten
2	tablespoons water

FOR THE FILLING

300g	lean minced lamb
4	shallots, finely chopped
2	garlic cloves, crushed
1	Granny Smith apple, cored and grated
½	teaspoon ground cinnamon
½	teaspoon ground nutmeg
½	teaspoon ground ginger
½	large bunch of fresh coriander, finely chopped
1	tablespoon pomegranate molasses (see p. 249 for the recipe)
150g	pine nuts, roughly chopped
200g	fresh spinach

To make the pastry

Blend the flour, butter and salt to coarse crumbs in a food processor. Add the egg yolk, yoghurt, water and cumin seeds and pulse again. Turn the mixture into a bowl and knead into a smooth dough. Cover and rest for 30 minutes in the fridge.

To make the filling

Combine the lamb, shallots, garlic, grated apple, cinnamon, nutmeg, ginger, fresh coriander, molasses and pine nuts in a bowl, and season to taste.

Meanwhile, bring a saucepan of water to boil and blanch the spinach for just a minute. Drain immediately and squeeze dry when cool enough to handle. Chop roughly, add to the meat and thoroughly combine.

To cook the pastries

Preheat the oven to 200°C fan/gas mark 7.

Take the pastry dough from the fridge and allow to stand at room temperature for 10 minutes. Then divide the pastry into 3 pieces. Roll each piece to a 0.5cm thickness, and cut into approximately 8cm circles, using a cutter or a cup.

Place a tablespoon of filling in the centre of each circle, then pull up 3 edges of the pastry to create a pyramid shape. Repeat the same process with the rest of the dough and filling.

Mix the beaten egg yolk in a bowl with 2 tablespoons of water. Brush the pyramid pastries with the egg mixture and bake in the oven for 12–14 minutes, until golden brown.

MAKES 24

Creamy Feta and Caramelised Leek Filo Börek

Börek is a Turkish pastry, made with either filo or yufka *pastry, then stuffed with various fillings, such as cheese, vegetable or meat. It can be a perfect snack, light lunch or a main meal. From the days of my childhood I remember it as an eagerly anticipated afternoon snack, always accompanied by* ayran, *a Turkish yoghurt drink.*

3 leeks, finely sliced

2 garlic cloves, crushed

½ teaspoon sugar

10g butter

2 tablespoons olive oil

200ml chicken stock

1 bay leaf

200g feta, crumbled

50g pack of fresh oregano, finely chopped

8 sheets of filo pastry

melted butter, for brushing

2 tablespoons mixed hemp, poppy and black sesame seeds

Preheat the oven to 200°C fan/gas mark 7.

Sauté the leeks, garlic and sugar in the butter and olive oil for 4–5 minutes, constantly stirring. Add the stock and bay leaf, and season. Cook until reduced to a mushy consistency. Take off the heat and remove the bay leaf. Once cooled, transfer the mixture to a bowl and combine with the cheese and oregano.

Working with one sheet of filo pastry at a time, spread it out and cut lengthwise into thirds. Keep the pastry covered with a damp tea towel while you're not using it. Each strip will make one börek.

Brush the pastry with the melted butter and place a tablespoon of filling across the corner of one end. Fold this corner up and over to form a triangle, then over again, and so on until you have a triangular pastry parcel. Repeat this process with the rest of the pastry and filling.

Arrange the böreks on a tray. Brush them with more melted butter and sprinkle with the seeds. Cook in the oven for 20 minutes, until golden brown.

MAKES 24

Baba Ghanoush

This delicious baba ghanoush was served to me at the home of the Hakawati Abu Shadi. It is very similar to that which my own grandmother used to make; always a favourite, I never tire of it.

2 large aubergines

3 garlic cloves, crushed

3 tablespoons tahini

juice of 2 large lemons

½ teaspoon ground cumin

¼ teaspoon paprika

50g pack of fresh parsley, finely chopped

1 tablespoon black sesame seeds

¼ teaspoon pink peppercorns, crushed

Place the aubergines directly on a naked gas flame (or the electric ring if you are using electric) and, taking care, cook on a medium heat for 10–12 minutes, turning occasionally, so that the aubergines are chargrilled evenly. The skin will blacken and start blistering and the aubergines will become soft, not to mention that your kitchen will be filled with a wonderful smell. Alternatively, you can bake them in the oven for 20 minutes at 200°C fan/gas mark 7, but the flavour won't be quite the same. Once cooked, place the aubergines in a strong plastic bag and allow them to sweat, which will make them easier to peel.

Peel and chop the aubergines, discarding any uncooked pieces you might find. Place the chopped flesh into a sieve. Over a bowl, press down gently to get rid of as much liquid as possible. Discard the liquid. Tip the aubergine into a bowl and, using a fork, combine with the garlic, tahini, lemon juice, cumin and paprika. Pulsing in a food processor will result in a smoother mixture.

Stir in the parsley, and serve sprinkled with black sesame seeds and crushed pink peppercorns.

SERVES 6

Damascene Walnut Tarator

Tarator is a Turkish-style sauce, based on nuts and herbs, with a hint of garlic and olive oil, a sort of pesto. Tarator sauces are often served as an accompaniment to fish and grilled vegetable dishes. They can be prepared using walnuts, pine nuts, almonds or hazelnuts. This is absolutely delicious, and is so easy it almost makes itself!

50g **pack of fresh parsley, finely chopped**

100g **walnuts, finely chopped**

2 **tablespoons ground walnuts**

2 **tablespoons tahini**

2 **garlic cloves, crushed**

½ **teaspoon cayenne pepper**

juice of 1 small lemon

Put aside a little of the parsley. Combine all the ingredients to make a smooth paste. Sprinkle with the reserved parsley and serve.

MAKES 150G

Pumpkin and Za'atar Hummus

approx. 450g **pumpkin, peeled and seeds removed**

4 **tablespoons olive oil**

3 **garlic cloves, crushed**

3 **tablespoons lemon juice**

1 **tablespoon za'atar (see p. 250 for the recipe)**

3 **teaspoons ground cumin**

1 **tablespoon tahini**

1 **teaspoon tahini (extra)**

2 **tablespoons toasted pumpkin seeds**

Preheat the oven to 200°C fan/gas mark 7.

Cut the pumpkin into wedges. Place on a tray, drizzle with the olive oil, and season. Roast in the oven for about 35 minutes, until golden and soft. Remove from the oven and leave to cool.

In a bowl, roughly mash the cooled pumpkin with a fork. Add the garlic, lemon juice, za'atar, cumin and tahini, combine well, and season. Place in a serving dish. Drizzle with the extra tahini and sprinkle with toasted pumpkin seeds.

SERVES 6

Veal, Sour Cherry and Almond Stuffed Vine Leaves

FOR THE VINE LEAVES

50   vine leaves, fresh or
preserved, or a 300g packet
of vine leaves

FOR THE STUFFING

2   tablespoons olive oil

1   medium shallot, finely
chopped

400g   veal, finely minced

100g   long-grain rice

100ml   chicken stock

½   teaspoon ground cumin

80g   almond flakes

80g   dried sour cherries

½   large bunch of fresh parsley,
finely chopped

½   large bunch of fresh mint,
finely chopped

To prepare the vine leaves

If you can't find fresh vine leaves then use preserved, and make sure that they are washed and drained well. Select 40 good leaves and put the rest to one side. Boil a saucepan of water, remove from the heat and drop in the vine leaves to blanch. After 5 minutes, remove the leaves and pat dry with a thick paper towel.

To make the stuffing

Heat the olive oil in a deep pan over a medium heat and sauté the shallot for 3 minutes, until soft. Add the minced veal and cook until brown all over. Add the rice and chicken stock and simmer for roughly 10 minutes. Stir in the cumin, and season. When most of the liquid has been absorbed by the rice, mix in the almonds and sour cherries.

Turn off the heat, cover with a clean tea towel and a lid, and leave to stand for 10 minutes – it will continue to cook. This is a traditional method that always produces a fluffy pilaf. Remove the towel and lid, and finally stir in the chopped parsley and mint.

To cook the vine leaves

Lay out a cooled, blanched leaf, shiny side down, and place a small amount of the veal mixture in the centre – just enough to still be able to comfortably wrap the leaf around the mixture. Fold the bottom edge nearest you over the filling, then fold in the two sides and tightly roll away from you into a neat parcel.

Line the bottom of a medium-sized saucepan with 4 or 5 of the unblanched leaves that you put aside. Arrange the stuffed vine leaves, seam side down, in the prepared saucepan, keeping them nice and tight in layers. Arrange the remaining unblanched leaves on top of the stuffed parcels. Add just enough water to cover. Weigh the parcels down with a plate to keep them in place. Simmer on gentle heat for 45–50 minutes.

Serve cool, with plain yoghurt.

SERVES 6

Fennel and Feta Kofte
with Walnut Tarator

FOR THE WALNUT TARATOR

- 1 slice of bread, crusts removed
- 200g walnuts
- 2 small garlic cloves
- 50g pack of fresh parsley, roughly chopped
- Juice of 1 lemon
- 5 tablespoons olive oil

FOR THE KOFTE

- 1 large fennel bulb, finely shaved into transparently thin strips
- 1 teaspoon fennel seeds, toasted
- 8 spring onions, finely sliced
- 50g pack of fresh parsley, finely chopped
- 100g feta, crumbled
- 3 eggs
- 3–4 tablespoons plain flour
- 1 teaspoon baking powder
- 4 tablespoons olive oil

To make the walnut tarator

Soak the bread in a bowl of water. Remove, squeeze out any excess water, and blend in a food processor with the walnuts, garlic, parsley and lemon juice, until the mixture forms a smooth purée. Add the olive oil, season and refrigerate until needed.

To make the kofte

Combine the fennel, fennel seeds, spring onions, parsley, feta, eggs, flour and baking powder in a bowl, and season with black pepper. Roll the mixture into small patties. Heat the olive oil in a large pan and cook the kofte for 2–3 minutes on each side, just a few at a time. Remove from the pan and place on kitchen paper to drain.

Serve the kofte cold, with the walnut tarator.

SERVES 4

Beetroot Moutabel with Tahini and Toasted Orange Peel

A moutabel dip is a must on the Eastern Mediterranean mezze table. A traditional Syrian speciality, it was usually made with aubergine, but nowadays there are a variety of moutabels, such as beetroot, potato and courgette.

Beetroot moutabel is not only delicious but a truly spectacular dish to look at because of its vibrant colour.

approx. 500g	**medium beets, uncooked, scrubbed clean**
4	**tablespoons olive oil**
the peel of 3	**oranges**
juice of ½	**lemon**
2	**tablespoons tahini**
2	**tablespoons thick, plain yoghurt**

Preheat the oven to 200°C fan/gas mark 7.

Arrange the beetroot on a roasting tray. Drizzle with olive oil, season and roast in the oven for 45–50 minutes, until cooked.

Meanwhile, scatter the orange peel in a small non-stick frying pan and toast on a medium heat for roughly 1 minute. Leave to cool.

Remove the beets from the oven and peel the skins once cool enough to handle. Grate half the beets on the finer side of a grater. Place the other half in a food processor and purée, but only roughly. This gives the moutabel more texture. Mix the two in a bowl with the lemon, tahini and yoghurt, and season.

Serve the moutabel topped with the toasted orange peel.

SERVES 6

Courgette Moutabel

This is a speciality of Al Halabi, Four Seasons, in Damascus, a restaurant that to my mind produces the best regional food in Aleppo.

3 **medium courgettes**

4 **tablespoons olive oil**

juice of ½ **lemon**

2 **tablespoons tahini**

2 **tablespoons plain yoghurt**

50g **pack of fresh parsley, finely chopped**

Slice the courgettes lengthwise as thinly as you can manage, using a mandolin if you have one. Fry the courgette slices in the olive oil for roughly 1 minute on each side, until golden brown.

Transfer the slices on to kitchen paper to drain, then place them in a bowl and roughly mash them with the lemon juice, tahini, yoghurt and parsley.

SERVES 6

Sujuk Sausage Roll

Sujuk is a type of spicy sausage that is often eaten in the cooler months. I clearly remember my father making it just before Christmas – it was heavenly. His was made with pork, but in countries like Syria and Turkey it is often prepared with lamb or beef.

This is another recipe that has endless variations, but here I have used the sujuk with puff pastry to create a type of Eastern Mediterranean sausage roll.

500g **minced lamb**

2 **garlic cloves, crushed**

1 **teaspoon ground cumin**

¼ **teaspoon ground nutmeg**

¼ **teaspoon ground cinnamon**

½ **teaspoon ground coriander**

1 **teaspoon mint**

1 **teaspoon oregano**

½ **teaspoon chilli flakes**

1 **teaspoon paprika**

500g **puff pastry**

1 **egg yolk, beaten**

3 **tablespoons hemp seeds**

Preheat the oven to 200°C fan/gas mark 7.

Combine the lamb, garlic, spices and dried herbs, and season. If you have a mincer, pass the mixture through at least twice.

Roll the puff pastry to roughly 0.5cm thickness, and shape into a square. Cut into long strips, roughly 6–8cm wide, and arrange a long, thin layer of the sausage mixture down the centre of each strip. Roll and seal the sausage meat within the pastry, so that the long edges of the pastry join up. Use a little water along the edges to help them stick together. Cut each sausage roll into 3cm pieces so you end up with bite-sized sausage rolls. Brush the top of each sausage roll with egg yolk and sprinkle with hemp seeds. Arrange on baking trays lined with greaseproof baking paper and cook in the oven for 20–25 minutes, until golden brown.

Tahini and Black Sesame Bread Swirls

These moist, almost cake-like bread swirls are fun and easy to prepare at home and best eaten warm. I enjoyed them served with cake in the humble home of Abu Shadi; his wife had just made them for their lunch. Her version was rather spice-heavy, so I have slightly adjusted the cinnamon and completely removed the cloves and nutmeg she used.

3	tablespoons warm water
1	teaspoon dry active yeast
300g	sugar
500g	plain flour
2	teaspoons ground cinnamon
2	teaspoons salt
2	tablespoons olive oil
3–4	tablespoons water
200g	tahini
3	tablespoons black sesame seeds

Mix the warm water and yeast in a bowl. Add a tablespoon of sugar, stir and set aside for roughly 10 minutes until it becomes frothy.

In a separate bowl, combine the flour, cinnamon and salt. Add the yeast mixture, 2 tablespoons of olive oil and 3–4 tablespoons water, stirring to make a rough dough. Turn the dough out of the bowl and knead on a floured surface for 8–10 minutes, until smooth and elastic. Return the dough to the bowl, cover with clingfilm, and leave to rise for 2 hours. Then divide the dough into 2 balls, cover again and allow to rise for a further 10 minutes.

Preheat the oven to 180°C fan/gas mark 6.

Roll each dough ball into a thin 60cm diameter circle. Evenly spread the tahini over the dough circles, then sprinkle the remaining sugar and the sesame seeds over the tahini.

Make a 2–3cm hole in the centre of each circle and with your fingers roll inwards the inner lip of the dough hole towards the outer edge of the circle, creating a large rolled-up rope ring, with the tahini, sugar and seeds enclosed within. An unusual technique but this is how it's been done for centuries!

Cut the rope into 6 equal lengths. Tightly coil each rope so that it resembles a cinnamon roll, then slightly flatten. Arrange on a baking tray lined with greaseproof baking paper and cook in the oven for 20 minutes.

Serve warm with hummus or jam.

MAKES 12

Avocado and Sumac Whip

This recipe is based on the principle of hummus preparation, only instead of chickpeas I have used velvety avocado, with a touch of nutty tahini and zesty sumac. While shooting the images for the book in Istanbul, I cooked a dinner for some Turkish friends and I prepared this very whip. They all loved it and declared it to be the Turkish version of guacamole, so you can best describe it like that, I guess!

2	**ripe avocados**
juice of 1	**small lemon**
3	**tablespoons olive oil**
4	**tablespoons tahini**
¼	**teaspoon ground cinnamon**
¼	**teaspoon ground cumin**
½	**teaspoon crushed or ground sumac**
3	**garlic cloves, crushed**
1	**tablespoon black sesame seeds**

Peel and cube the avocados, discarding the stones. Blend with the lemon juice in a food processor until smooth. Add the olive oil, tahini, cinnamon, cumin, sumac and garlic and mix together until it's the consistency of mayonnaise.

Sprinkle with the sesame seeds and serve.

SERVES 4

STARTERS

On the southern side of the Galata Bridge a great crowd of locals queue to buy a token to get them on to the Eminönü quayside for the twenty-minute trip across the Bosphorus from Europe into Asia.

On a wonderfully sunny afternoon, amid the smell of fried fish, I join the queue, buy my token, and leap aboard the ferry just as the diesel engines roar and the gangplank is pulled in. The boat slips into the wide stream, the gulls scream and all manner of boat sirens give herald to our movement out into one of the world's busiest shipping lanes. I'm treated to a wondrous view of the Topkapi Palace and the minarets of the Blue Mosque, a sight that I have seen many times, but of which I will never tire. The fishy smoke follows us out across the water and slowly fades to be replaced by the salty tang of the sea.

The reason for my trip was to visit my favourite eateries, the Çiya restaurants of Kadýköy, three restaurants in the same street

in the fish market district that produce the most wonderful Anatolian cuisine. I was to meet with Musa Daðdeviren, the founder and owner.

Musa was born in Nizip in eastern Turkey, into a family of bakers and chefs. He came to Istanbul twenty years ago, with the belief that traditional Anatolian cooking needed to be resurrected before it became overwhelmed by the fast food outlets that were springing up across Turkey's biggest city.

Over a traditional baba ghanoush I asked Musa what the name Çiya meant. He explained that it had three separate meanings: a wild flower from the mountains on the borders of Turkey and Syria; the sound of feet as they hit the floor during a traditional Georgian dance; and an old Turkish word for the sparkle of a fire. Each meaning is so wonderfully evocative and such a summing up of what this cuisine has to offer, that Çiya could not be better named.

King Prawn and Blood Orange Charmola Salad

This is a refreshingly light summer salad inspired by the Ottoman influence in North Africa. The blood orange season is short, but it can be made with any oranges.

12 large fresh king prawns, shells and heads removed

2 large blood oranges, peeled and segmented

2 large shallots, chopped

1 garlic clove, chopped

4 tablespoons olive oil

1 teaspoon ground cumin

1 teaspoon paprika

2 cm piece of fresh root ginger, peeled and finely chopped

8 sun-dried tomatoes, soaked in warm water for 30 minutes

½ large bunch of fresh coriander, roughly chopped

Cook the prawns in a large saucepan of boiling water for 3–4 minutes, drain and cool. Place the prawns and oranges in a large bowl.

Combine the shallots, garlic, olive oil, cumin, paprika, ginger and sun-dried tomatoes in a food processor and blend until you have a smooth paste. Add the paste to the prawns and oranges. Toss together and season. Sprinkle with the coriander and serve with crusty bread.

SERVES 4

Chickpea and Courgette Kofte with Mulberry and Chive Flower Salad

Kofte is a meatball, often mixed with rice or bulgur; it can be fried, baked or grilled. Turkish cuisine has over 300 types of kofte. I was brought up with my mother's special kofte, which she made almost daily, and it was and still is my perfect fast food. This particular recipe is a vegetarian version and bulgur is used to bind the mixture, so using finely ground bulgur is very important. If you can't find fresh mulberries, then use any dried berries or pomegranate seeds.

FOR THE KOFTE

- 7 tablespoons olive oil
- 1 medium red onion, peeled and finely grated
- 1 courgette, grated
- ½ teaspoon sweet paprika
- 1 teaspoon hot paprika
- 1 teaspoon ground cumin
- 200g dried chickpeas, soaked overnight
- 800ml water
- 50g finely ground bulgur
- 2 tablespoons plain flour, for dusting

To make the kofte

In a large saucepan, heat 3 tablespoons of olive oil and add the onion and courgette. Season and cook for roughly 3 minutes, until tender, stirring constantly. Add the paprikas and cumin and stir well.

Drain the chickpeas, add to the onions and courgettes, then pour in the water and bring to the boil. Reduce to a simmer and cook for 15–20 minutes, until almost three quarters of the liquid has been absorbed. Cool the mixture a little, then tip into a food processor, pulsing so that the mixture is crushed but not puréed. Stir in the bulgur, which will absorb the remaining liquid. Leave to stand for 15 minutes, then season.

To make the salad

Follow the packet instructions for cooking the bulgur and leave to cool.

Combine the onion, cooled cooked bulgur, mulberries, molasses, lemon juice and olive oil in a large bowl, and season. Mix in the chives, then scatter over the toasted almonds and fresh chive flowers.

FOR THE SALAD

50g **finely ground bulgur**

1 **small red onion, thinly sliced**

6–8 **fresh mulberries or the seeds from 1 small pomegranate**

1 **tablespoon pomegranate molasses (see p. 249 for the recipe)**

1 **tablespoon lemon juice**

2 **tablespoons olive oil**

½ **large bunch of fresh chives, finely chopped**

2 **tablespoons toasted sliced almonds**

6–8 **fresh chive flowers**

To cook the kofte

When the kofte mixture is completely cooled, mould it into patties by scooping roughly 2 tablespoons at a time and shaping it between your hands. Dust lightly with flour, and pan-fry on a medium to high heat in 2–4 tablespoons of olive oil for roughly 1 minute on each side. Place on kitchen paper to drain, and serve warm with the mulberry and chive flower salad.

SERVES 6

Sumac Braised Nettles
Topped with Onion Seeds

Nettles are the original free and wild food! Used mainly in soups, they are loaded with iron and exceptionally good to eat. Once blanched, they no longer sting. I remember my grandmother making wonderfully warming and vivid green nettle soup with a poached egg and a sprinkle of paprika.

Wear gloves when collecting nettles. In spring and summer they're everywhere. Try to pick the younger shoots on top of the plant and gather roughly a carrier bag full. Back home, trim the nettles, keeping only the leaves and discarding the stems. If you can't get hold of nettles, watercress or spinach works almost as well.

300g	**freshly picked nettle leaves**
500ml	**hot water**
3	**tablespoons olive oil**
6	**spring onions, finely sliced**
1	**garlic clove, crushed**
150g	**white long-grain rice**
½	**teaspoon crushed or ground sumac**
1	**teaspoon toasted onion seeds**
100g	**feta**

Wearing gloves, place the nettles in a saucepan and pour over 500ml of hot water. Boil for 1–2 minutes, until wilted, then drain but keep a cupful of the leftover water.

In a large saucepan gently heat the olive oil. Sauté the spring onions and garlic for 2–3 minutes. Add the rice, stirring to ensure the grains are well coated with the oil. Finally, add the wilted nettles and the reserved cupful of water. Cover and simmer for 10–12 minutes, until the rice is soft and all the liquid has been absorbed. Season, sprinkle with the sumac, stir well and serve topped with the toasted onion seeds and a wedge of feta on the side.

SERVES 4

Poached Eggs with a Yoghurt and Paprika Dressing

There are so many reasons why I miss my father, too many to recount. One thing that will remain with me always is the way he would whip up a delicious dish out of thin air, and how we would sit at the old wooden table outside our villa in the mountains and with some local bread in hand, a tasty meal in front of us, we would talk, nothing special, just chit-chat, and listen to the cowbells ringing in the distance. It was idyllic, something I will never forget.

This extremely simple dish was one of his favourites, but I make no excuse for including it. The Turkish love it and call it gilbir.

4	**tablespoons vinegar**
8	**eggs**
400ml	**yoghurt**
4–5	**fresh mint sprigs, finely chopped**

TO SERVE À LA TURQUE (optional)

1	**garlic clove, crushed**
30g	**butter**
4	**teaspoons paprika**

Half fill a saucepan with salted water and add the vinegar. Bring to the boil and turn down the heat so that it is just roughly simmering. The water must not be boiling vigorously.

One at a time, crack the eggs into a small bowl and gently slide them into the simmering water. Do not cook more than 2 at a time. If an egg seems to be going wrong and isn't keeping its shape, scoop it out with a spoon and start again. You'll need to cook the eggs for 3–4 minutes for a soft yolk, and at least 5 minutes for a hard yolk.

Remove the eggs with a slotted spoon. Pour the yoghurt over the top of the eggs, season and serve with a sprinkle of chopped mint.

To serve à la Turque

As an alternative, and this I highly recommend, make the yoghurt à la Turque by stirring in the garlic. Then heat the butter until it's sizzling, and sauté the paprika for ½ minute (don't let it burn), then pour this over the eggs and garlic yoghurt.

SERVES 4

Cannellini Beans and Za'atar Sautéed Mushrooms on Toast

300g	dried cannellini beans, soaked overnight
juice of 1	lemon
4	tablespoons single cream
1	tablespoon tahini
2	tablespoons olive oil
250g	field mushrooms, sliced
4	garlic cloves, crushed
3	tablespoons za'atar (see p. 250 for the recipe)
1	teaspoon black sesame seeds
4	slices of crusty bread, toasted

Drain the beans, then cook them in boiling water for 45–60 minutes, until tender. Drain and purée in a food processor. Fold in the lemon juice, single cream and tahini, and season.

Heat the oil in a frying pan and sauté the mushrooms and garlic until browned. Add the za'atar and sesame seeds and stir.

Spoon the cannellini bean purée on to the toasted bread slices and top with the sautéed mushrooms. Serve drizzled with a little tahini if desired.

SERVES 4

Mahluta – Lentil, Rice and Lamb Soup

I was brought up on soups; light broths, meatball soups, yoghurt soups, vegetable soups, but most of all lentil soups. With a nod to modesty, I think I'm a bit of an expert on this subject, so I was absolutely delighted to discover a lentil-based soup at the Al Halabi, Four Seasons, in Damascus that I hadn't yet tried. Delicious and fragrant doesn't begin to do it justice.

250g **red lentils**

50g **short-grain rice**

2 **tablespoons olive oil**

1 **onion, grated**

2 **garlic cloves, crushed**

2 **tablespoons ground cumin**

150g **lean minced lamb**

1 **small coconut, peeled**

Place the lentils and rice in a saucepan, add 1.5 litres of water, and season. Bring to the boil, then reduce to a simmer.

Gently heat a little olive oil in a frying pan and sauté the onion, garlic and cumin for a few minutes. Add the lamb and cook for 5 minutes, or until brown all over. Spoon the lamb mixture into the lentil and rice pan and simmer for roughly 30 minutes, until the lentils and rice are cooked.

Meanwhile, shave the coconut into paper-thin slices. Place in a dry pan over a medium to high heat and toast until golden brown. Put aside to cool.

Serve the soup topped with the toasted coconut.

SERVES 6

Saffron and Lemon Soup with Lobster

For this Eastern Mediterranean version of bouillabaisse, any chunky meaty fish will do. Monkfish works particularly well, but lobster makes it a very special dish indeed. Or you can use king prawns – just add 200g of raw shelled king prawns during the last 5–6 minutes of cooking time.

450g	lobster, cooked
1.5kg	fish bones, for the stock
2	shallots, halved
2	bay leaves
1	garlic clove, peeled and whole
3	celery sticks, chopped
1	carrot, chopped
½	small fennel bulb, chopped
pinch of	saffron
2	ripe tomatoes, chopped
6	fresh thyme sprigs, chopped
200ml	dry white wine
50g	fine vermicelli, chopped
4	large egg yolks
juice of 2	lemons
50g	pack of fresh parsley, finely chopped

Shell and break the lobster meat into bite-sized pieces. Set aside for later.

Place the fish bones, shallots, bay leaves, garlic, celery, carrot and fennel in a large saucepan and cover with water. Season, bring to the boil, then reduce to a simmer and cook on a low heat for 20 minutes. Strain the liquid into a saucepan and keep this, as it's now your soup stock. Discard the solids.

To the stock, add the saffron, tomatoes, thyme, white wine and vermicelli. Cook on a low heat for 8–10 minutes, until the vermicelli is cooked.

In a small bowl, whisk the egg yolks and lemon juice, then ladle 300ml of the cooked soup into the eggs and lemon, not the other way round, and stir. Now add the egg and lemon mixture to the soup. Briefly simmer for 1–2 minutes to cook the egg.

Pour the soup into bowls, add the lobster pieces, and serve sprinkled with parsley.

SERVES 6

Pistachio and Sumac Crumbed Scallops with Pistachio Sauce

FOR THE SAUCE

100g	pistachios, roughly chopped
	large bunch of fresh parsley, roughly chopped
juice of	1 small lemon
100ml	olive oil

FOR THE SCALLOPS

80g	whole pistachios, shelled
1	teaspoon sumac, ground to a powder
1	tablespoon onion seeds
12	large scallops
	melted butter, for brushing
1	tablespoon olive oil

To make the sauce

Process the pistachios, parsley and lemon juice in a blender, drizzling in the olive oil a little at a time until you have a smooth, thick consistency, and season.

To cook the scallops

In a dry pan, lightly toast the pistachios over a medium to high heat. Allow to cool before placing in a food processor and grinding down to a powdery consistency. Tip into a bowl and combine with the sumac and onion seeds. Brush each scallop with melted butter and roll in the pistachio mixture.

Heat the olive oil in a griddle pan on a medium to high heat and sear the scallops for 2–3 minutes on each side, so that they turn golden brown.

Arrange 3 scallops on each serving plate and drizzle with the pistachio sauce.

SERVES 4

Herb Marinated Goat's Cheese in Grilled Vine Leaves Served with Thyme and Garlic Brioche

Goat's cheese and vine leaves: nothing could be more Eastern Mediterranean. Simple, light and delicious!

FOR THE GOAT'S CHEESE

400g	**soft goat's cheese**
200ml	**olive oil**
50g	**pack of fresh dill, finely chopped**
50g	**pack of fresh thyme, finely chopped**
50g	**pack of fresh basil, finely chopped**
2	**garlic cloves, peeled and whole**
24	**medium vine leaves**

FOR THE BRIOCHE

6	**tablespoons clarified butter or ghee**
1	**garlic clove, crushed**
50g	**pack of fresh thyme, chopped**
4	**slices of brioche**

24 hours in advance

Divide the goat's cheese into 12 pieces, shape into discs and put into a large glass bowl. In a separate bowl combine the olive oil, dill, thyme and basil. Throw in the whole garlic cloves and pour the mixture over the goat's cheese. Cover and allow to marinate for 24 hours.

On the day

If you're using fresh vine leaves, blanch them in hot water for a couple of minutes and drain. If using preserved leaves, just wash thoroughly and drain. Lay out 2 vine leaves side by side, slightly overlapping them, shiny side down. Place a marinated goat's cheese disc in the centre. Fold the vine leaves in to enclose the cheese. Do this with all the goat's cheese discs.

Place the goat's cheese parcels under a medium to hot grill and cook for 2–3 minutes on each side, until they turn brown and evenly crisp.

To make the brioche

In a large frying pan, gently heat the butter with the crushed garlic and chopped thyme leaves. Stir and cook for 2–3 minutes. Place the slices of brioche in the pan and allow them to soak up the garlic butter, then cook for a minute on each side until lightly browned. Serve hot, with 3 vine-leaf parcels on each slice of brioche.

SERVES 4

'Through a gap in the rocks, my eye fell on the strangest and most fantastic sight which man has ever seen: it was Damascus and its boundless desert, a few hundred feet below my path…first the town, surrounded by its walls, a forest of minarets of all shapes, watered by the seven branches of its river, and streams without number, until the view is lost in a labyrinth of flower gardens and trees…'

Alphonse de Lamartine (1833)

Until very recently I was madly in love with the great mystical city of Istanbul. I thought that no place could be so grand, nor so steeped in history, and that love has not diminished, but a new light has come into my life: Damascus.

Damascus, one of the greatest cities in history, was already old when Rome was founded. Its heritage seeps from every wall, permeating the fabric of the city and the very bones of the citizens, the friendliest people that I have ever had the pleasure to meet. Damascus's dilapidated grandeur is absolutely magical, oozing surreal emotions and passions in dreamlike splendour.

It is no exaggeration to say that visiting Damascus brings me a sense of renewal. It is like waking from a night's sleep a day younger, not older. All the words in the world cannot describe this place. You need to go there to feel its soul and energy, for it is for ever young.

Veal Sweetbreads in Cumin, Sumac and Mustard Crumb

I originally had this dish in a small café on the Asian side of the Bosphorus, where it was served with lamb sweetbreads. Personally I think veal sweetbreads are superior in taste and texture, so that's why I suggest you use them.

600g **veal sweetbreads, trimmed of excess fat**

1 **carrot, chopped**

1 **small onion, chopped**

1 **celery stick, chopped**

200g **fine breadcrumbs**

1 **teaspoon mustard powder**

1 **teaspoon crushed or ground sumac**

1 **teaspoon ground cumin**

2–4 **tablespoons olive oil**

1 day in advance

Place the sweetbreads in a glass bowl and cover with cold water. Cover and allow to soak overnight.

On the day

Drain the sweetbreads and place them in a saucepan with the carrot, onion and celery. Cover with fresh water and bring to the boil. Reduce to a simmer and cook for 5 minutes, then drain and discard the vegetables. Place the sweetbreads on a plate and remove any excess membrane that may still be left.

In a bowl, combine the breadcrumbs, mustard, sumac and cumin, and season. Cut the sweetbreads into 3–4cm pieces, brush lightly with a little oil and roll them in the breadcrumb mixture until coated.

Heat the remaining oil in a non-stick pan and lightly sauté the breaded sweetbreads on all sides to brown evenly, roughly 30 seconds per side.

Serve with tomato, pomegranate and sumac salad (see p. 126 for the recipe).

SERVES 4

Cheddar, Coriander and Chard Gözleme

Gözleme are a favourite Turkish street food, little pastries stuffed with meat, vegetable or cheese, then fried or cooked on a griddle. We used to make them at home with a yellow cheese, known as kashkaval. *It is a mild hard cheese, available in Turkish or Middle Eastern shops. Using a mild Cheddar or Gruyère as a substitute works well too.*

2	**teaspoons olive oil**
500g	**Swiss chard leaves, chopped**
½	**large bunch of fresh coriander, leaves only, chopped**
1	**long red chilli, deseeded and finely chopped**
1	**red onion, grated**
2	**garlic cloves, crushed**
200g	**kashkaval or mild Cheddar, grated**
2	**large sheets of yufka or filo pastry**
4–5	**tablespoons clarified butter or ghee, melted**

In a large frying pan, heat the olive oil and sauté the chard, coriander, chilli, onion and garlic for 2–3 minutes, until the leaves have wilted. Remove from the heat, drain and discard any cooking juices. Cool in a glass bowl, then add the grated cheese.

As with filo pastry, yufka dries out very quickly so it must be covered with a damp cloth when you're not working. Usually yufka is available in rounds, so lay 2 of these sheets on top of each other, then cut into 6 equal-size wedges, giving you 12 in total. Now cut off the rounded edges at the top of each wedge so that you have triangles.

Working with one triangle at a time, spoon some of the chard and cheese filling into the middle and brush the sides with melted butter. Fold the points of the triangle so that they overlap and enclose the filling. Brush the tops with melted butter and arrange on a platter. Repeat until you have 12 filled pastries.

Heat the remaining butter in a non-stick pan and sauté the gözleme for 2–3 minutes on each side, until brown.

Serve hot or cold.

MAKES 12

Almond and Roasted Garlic Soup with Toasted Coconut

This soup is best prepared with fresh green almonds straight from their velvety shells. Just like walnuts, almonds harden after harvest, so most of us are only familiar with the almond once it has turned brittle and brown. When still green, the almond is milky and very sweet. The season for fresh almonds is short, so if you're unable to get hold of any, use good-quality whole blanched almonds.

4	whole garlic bulbs
10g	butter
1	tablespoon olive oil
6	shallots, thinly sliced
2	slices of brioche
230g	fresh or blanched almonds
400ml	chicken stock
½	coconut, peeled and grated

Preheat the oven to 180°C fan/gas mark 6.

Place the garlic bulbs on a small baking tray and roast in the oven for 30–40 minutes, until the garlic is soft. Remove and set aside to cool, leaving the oven on.

In a saucepan, heat the butter and oil on a low heat and gently sauté the shallots for 8–10 minutes, making sure they don't brown but become soft and mushy. Remove from the heat. Squeeze the garlic out of its skin, like squeezing toothpaste from a tube, and stir in to the sautéed shallots.

Cut the brioche into 1cm cubes. Spread the brioche cubes and almonds out on a baking tray lined with greaseproof baking paper. Cook in the oven for 10 minutes until they've just turned a light golden brown. Remove and set aside to cool. Meanwhile, bring the chicken stock to the boil in a large saucepan.

Put the cooled almonds and brioche in a food processor and blitz until they're finely ground. Add half the hot stock and slowly process until you have a thick purée. Transfer the mixture to the remaining stock in the saucepan and stir well to combine. Add the shallots and garlic and again stir to combine. Simmer for a few more minutes, until you have a silky smooth, puréed soup.

Toast the coconut in a dry non-stick frying pan on a medium to high heat, until golden. Allow to cool.

Serve the soup topped with the toasted coconut.

SERVES 6

Chilled Sweet Pea and Watercress Soup with Rose Petal Cream

FOR THE SOUP

150g	**fresh watercress leaves**
1	**small onion, grated**
950ml	**water**
900g	**fresh peas**
50g	**pack of fresh parsley, finely chopped**
50g	**pack of fresh thyme, leaves only**
50g	**pack of fresh chervil, finely chopped**
	large bowl filled with ice cubes

FOR THE CREAM

2	**large red or pink roses (washed)**
150g	**double cream**
pinch of	**ground pink peppercorns**

To make the soup

Place the watercress and onion in a saucepan and add 150ml of water. Bring to the boil, then reduce to a simmer and cook for just 1 minute. Now add the peas, parsley, thyme and chervil. Pour in a further 800ml of water, season and bring back to the boil. Reduce the heat and simmer for 3 minutes.

To stop the soup overcooking, pour it straight into a bowl and sit this in the bowl of ice cubes. Allow to cool completely, then purée in a food processor and pass through a fine sieve.

To make the cream

Pick off the rose petals, wash them and put half a dozen or so to one side for the garnish. Place the rest of the petals in a food processor and purée.

Whisk the cream until thickened and add to the rose purée, season with salt and add a pinch of pink peppercorns.

To serve

Serve the soup with a dollop of the rose petal cream and scattered with the reserved rose petals.

SERVES 4

Yoghurt and Oregano Pesto Soup with Oregano Flowers

Eaten throughout Turkey, this soup is especially popular in Anatolia and is also found in Syria. It is served hot, most often flavoured with mint, cornflour being used to stabilise the yoghurt. Here I have used oregano instead of mint. As it is a seasonal soup, made with fresh oregano, I love using the flowers of the plant too!

FOR THE OREGANO PESTO

	large bunch of fresh oregano, leaves and flowers
2	garlic cloves, crushed
100g	pine nuts
4	tablespoons olive oil
3	tablespoons Parmesan, grated

FOR THE SOUP

1	tablespoon olive oil
1	celery stick, chopped
1	carrot, chopped
½	onion, chopped
3–4	sprigs of fresh thyme
1	bay leaf
3–4	sprigs of fresh oregano
1.2 litres	chicken stock
2	tablespoons risotto rice
1	tablespoon cornflour
450g	thick yoghurt, strained
2	egg yolks
1	teaspoon chilli flakes
100g	cooked chickpeas

To make the oregano pesto

Put aside some of the oregano flowers for the garnish. Using a pestle and mortar, make a chunky paste with the oregano and garlic (or use a food processor if you prefer a smoother paste), then add the pine nuts and grind. Finally, add the olive oil and Parmesan and combine well. If you would like your pesto to have a little thinner consistency, add a touch more olive oil. Refrigerate until needed.

To make the soup

In a large saucepan, heat the olive oil and cook the celery, carrot and onion for 2–3 minutes. Add the thyme, bay leaf and oregano, and season. Now pour in the chicken stock. Simmer gently for 15 minutes, then strain into another saucepan and discard the solids. Add the rice to the strained stock and cook for 30 minutes, until tender.

Spoon a tablespoon of cornflour into a small bowl, add a little of the soup and mix well. Pour the yoghurt into a separate bowl and add 2–3 tablespoons of soup, beat for a moment, then add the egg yolks and the cornflour mixture. Stir well.

Pour the yoghurt mixture into the soup and cook over a low to medium heat so that it is barely simmering. Take care not to let it boil, as this will curdle the yoghurt.

Add the chilli flakes, and season.

To serve

Serve hot in large deep dishes. Put a small handful of chickpeas in the middle, top with a spoonful of the oregano pesto, and finish with the fresh oregano flowers.

SERVES 6–8

Egg and Lemon Soup with Fresh Crab and Lemon Balm

Nothing speaks more of the Eastern Mediterranean than the lemon and, personally speaking, I will add lemon juice to almost any fish or soup dish. Eggs and lemon, or terbiye, can also be cooked with rice rather than orzo. Adding lemon balm gives an extra lemony flavour.

1 litre	light chicken stock
6	tablespoons orzo pasta
4	egg yolks
zest and juice of 1	large lemon
100g	wild rocket
300g	fresh white crabmeat, cooked
½	teaspoon crushed or ground sumac
4–5	sprigs of fresh lemon balm, leaves only, finely chopped

Bring the chicken stock to the boil in a large saucepan over a medium heat, then reduce the heat, add the orzo and simmer for 25 minutes.

Combine the egg yolks, lemon juice and zest in a bowl. Mix in 50–100ml of the hot stock, then pour the mixture into the saucepan and stir. Season and add the rocket. Simmer for a further 3–4 minutes. Finally, add the crabmeat and cook for a further minute, until heated through.

Remove from the heat and serve topped with a sprinkle of sumac and chopped lemon balm.

SERVES 6–8

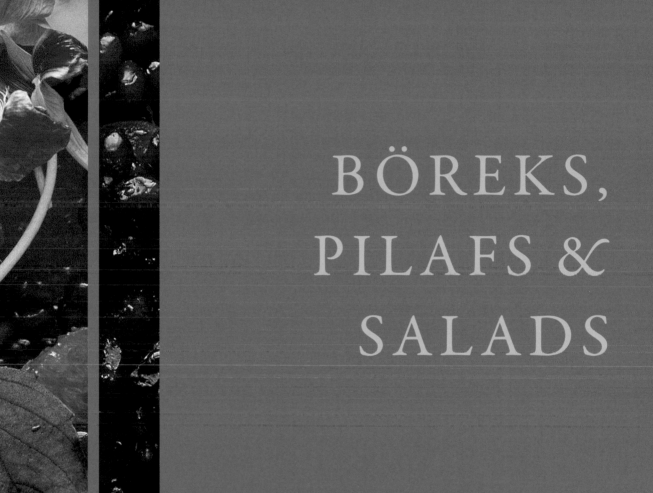

BÖREKS, PILAFS & SALADS

Börek

Börek is quintessentially Turkish! Some of the best böreks in the world are served from stalls on the street corners of Turkey and Syria. They are light, fluffy, crispy pastries filled with whatever the season has brought to the kitchen. Usually made with either filo or yufka pastry, they can also be prepared with yoghurt-based flaky pastry or puff pastry.

Sweet Potato and Spring Onion Börek

2 **large sweet potatoes, peeled and cubed**

10g **butter**

6 **spring onions, finely sliced**

½ **teaspoon paprika**

½ **tablespoon onion seeds**

4 **large sheets of filo pastry**
   melted butter, for brushing

1 **egg yolk, beaten**

1 **teaspoon onion seeds**

Preheat the oven to 190°C fan/gas mark 6½.

Place the sweet potatoes in a saucepan of cold water and bring to the boil, then reduce to a simmer for 12–15 minutes, until the potatoes are soft. Drain and roughly mash the potatoes – you don't want them to be too smooth.

Heat the butter in a deep saucepan and sauté the spring onions for 1 minute, then add the warm mashed potatoes, paprika and onion seeds. Combine well.

Place a sheet of filo pastry on your work surface and brush with melted butter, then immediately place another sheet of filo on top of the first. Spoon half the potato mixture along the bottom edge of the filo sheets, roll away from you to form a thin sausage and tuck the ends in. Repeat the process with the other 2 filo sheets. Filo can dry quickly, so keep the pastry that you are not using under a damp cloth.

Arrange the 2 böreks on a baking tray, brush with the beaten egg and sprinkle with onion seeds. Bake in the oven for 12–15 minutes, until golden. Cut up and serve warm. Simple and delicious!

SERVES 6

Lentil and Swiss Chard Börek

FOR THE PASTRY

400g **self-raising flour**

80g **cold butter, cubed**

1 **egg yolk**

2 **tablespoons water**

80ml **crème fraiche**

¼ **teaspoon salt**

plain flour, for dusting

1 **small egg yolk, for brushing**

1 **tablespoon white sesame seeds**

FOR THE FILLING

2 **tablespoons olive oil**

6 **spring onions, finely sliced**

200g **Swiss chard, chopped**

80g **green lentils, cooked**

Preheat the oven to 180°C fan/gas mark 6.

To make the pastry

Combine the flour and butter in a food processor, until you have coarse crumbs. Add the egg yolk, water, crème fraiche and salt and pulse to get a soft, smooth dough. Cover and refrigerate for 30 minutes.

To make the filling

Meanwhile, heat the oil in a large frying pan and sauté the spring onions for 2 minutes. Add the Swiss chard and cook for a further 2 minutes, then add the lentils and remove from the heat. Season and leave to cool.

To cook the börek

Remove the dough from the fridge and let it rest at room temperature for 10 minutes. Dust a clean surface with flour and roll out the dough to roughly 40cm square, about 1cm thick. Cut the pastry into 5 horizontal strips, then cut in the opposite direction to make 25 equal squares.

Brush the edges of each square with the egg yolk mixed with a few drops of water – egg wash. Place a small amount of the filling in the centre of each square. For each square, lift one corner and fold it to the diagonally opposite corner. Seal the edges to encase the filling so that you have triangular-shaped parcels. Brush the top of each parcel with a little more egg wash then arrange the parcels on a baking tray, sprinkle with the sesame seeds and bake in the oven for 25–30 minutes, until golden brown.

MAKES 25

Wild Greens and Feta Börek

Use any wild greens that are available, or use spinach or watercress instead.

2	tablespoons olive oil
200g	nettles (for more on nettles, see p. 76)
300g	wild rocket
200g	feta, crumbled
½	teaspoon ground black pepper
½	teaspoon cayenne pepper
2	eggs
250ml	milk
6	tablespoons melted butter
20	sheets of filo pastry
2	tablespoons nigella seeds

Preheat the oven to 200°C fan/gas mark 7.

Heat the olive oil in a saucepan and sauté the nettles (don't forget to use gloves) and rocket for 2 minutes, until just wilted. With your hands, thoroughly squeeze dry the greens and place them in a large bowl. Add the feta and the black and cayenne pepper, and combine.

In another bowl beat the eggs then stir in the milk and melted butter. Oil a 10 × 20cm baking tray. Line the tray with a sheet of filo pastry, brush it generously with the egg mixture, then top with another sheet and repeat the process until you have used half the filo sheets.

Now spoon in the greens and feta mixture and top with the remaining filo sheets as before, brushing with the egg mixture between each layer. Pour any remaining egg mixture over the final layer and sprinkle with nigella seeds.

Bake in the oven for 30–35 minutes or until golden brown. Remove and set aside to cool.

Cut into diamond shapes and serve.

SERVES 8

Pilaf

The pilaf is the emperor of rice dishes: exquisite, seductive, light, velvety and simply irresistible! Traditionally the best rice to use is baldo, which is readily available, but arborio rice can be substituted.

Wild Rice Pilaf with Spinach and Broad Beans

400g	**fresh broad beans, unshelled**
200g	**wild rice, soaked in cold water for 12 hours**
30g	**butter**
1	**onion, finely chopped**
1	**litre vegetable stock**
400g	**fresh spinach, chopped**
50g	**pack of fresh parsley, chopped**
zest of 1	**lemon**
80g	**pine nuts, lightly toasted**

TO SERVE

200g	**yoghurt**
2	**tablespoons olive oil**
	sweet paprika

Shell the broad beans and drop them into a pan of boiling water. Simmer for 3–5 minutes, then drain and cool. Once cooled, remove the outer skins.

Drain the rice – I pre-soak it as this makes it easier to cook. Heat the butter in a saucepan and sauté the onion for 3–4 minutes, then add the drained rice and cook for a further 2 minutes, stirring all the time. Season and add the vegetable stock. Bring everything to the boil, cover and simmer on a low heat for 20–35 minutes, until the rice is almost cooked. Then add the spinach, broad beans, parsley, lemon zest and pine nuts.

To serve

Fluff the rice with a fork and serve with a dollop of yoghurt, a drizzle of olive oil and a sprinkle of sweet paprika.

SERVES 4

Pilaf with Vermicelli, Chickpeas, Apricots and Pistachios

This is street food, Turkish style. This dish can be found in the markets of Istanbul, sold as a hot lunch, often topped with freshly boiled chicken breast.

2	shallots, sliced
20g	clarified butter or ghee
80g	vermicelli
100g	cooked chickpeas
80g	dried apricots, chopped
300g	baldo rice or short-grain rice
400ml	vegetable stock
80g	pistachios, roughly chopped

In a saucepan, sauté the shallots in the butter for 2 minutes on a medium heat. Add the vermicelli and, continually stirring, cook until golden, keeping an eye on it because this happens pretty quickly. Add the chickpeas, apricots and the rice, making sure the rice is well coated with the butter. Pour in the stock and bring to the boil. Reduce to a simmer, season and cover with a lid. Cook on a low heat for 15–20 minutes, without stirring. Have a look from time to time to see if you need to add a little more liquid.

When the rice is cooked, add the pistachios and turn off the heat. Cover the saucepan with a clean cloth and replace the lid. Allow to rest for 15–20 minutes – this will allow the rice to cook further while becoming lovely and fluffy.

SERVES 4

Kadirga Pilaf with Pistachios, Almonds and Currants, Topped with Béchamel Sauce

FOR THE PILAF

- 2 **tablespoons butter**
- 2 **shallots, grated**
- 2 **garlic cloves, crushed**
- 100g **organic currants**
- 250g **baldo rice or short-grain rice**
- 400ml **good-quality chicken stock**
- 70g **unsalted shelled pistachios, roughly chopped**
- 60g **unsalted blanched almonds, roughly chopped**
- ½ **large bunch of fresh oregano, finely chopped**
- ½ **large bunch of fresh parsley, finely chopped**

FOR THE BÉCHAMEL SAUCE

- 2 **tablespoons butter**
- 1½ **tablespoons plain flour**
- 250ml **milk**
- ½ **teaspoon ground nutmeg**
- 100g **gruyère, grated**

Preheat the oven to 200°C fan/gas mark 7.

To make the pilaf

Melt the butter in an ovenproof casserole dish over a medium heat. Sauté the shallots, garlic and currants in the butter for 1 minute, then add the rice, coating thoroughly. Pour in the stock, then cover and cook for 12–15 minutes on a very low heat. Remove from the heat, add the pistachios, almonds, oregano and parsley, and combine well.

To make the béchamel sauce

Heat the butter in a small saucepan over a medium-low heat until melted. Add the flour, stirring all the time until it combines to a smooth paste. Whisk in the milk, adding a little at a time, then add the nutmeg, and season. Cook on a low heat for 5 minutes, taking care not to let it boil. Finally, add the cheese and stir until it has all melted into the sauce.

Pour the sauce over the pilaf and transfer to the oven for 5 minutes, until the top is golden.

Serve hot.

SERVES 4–6

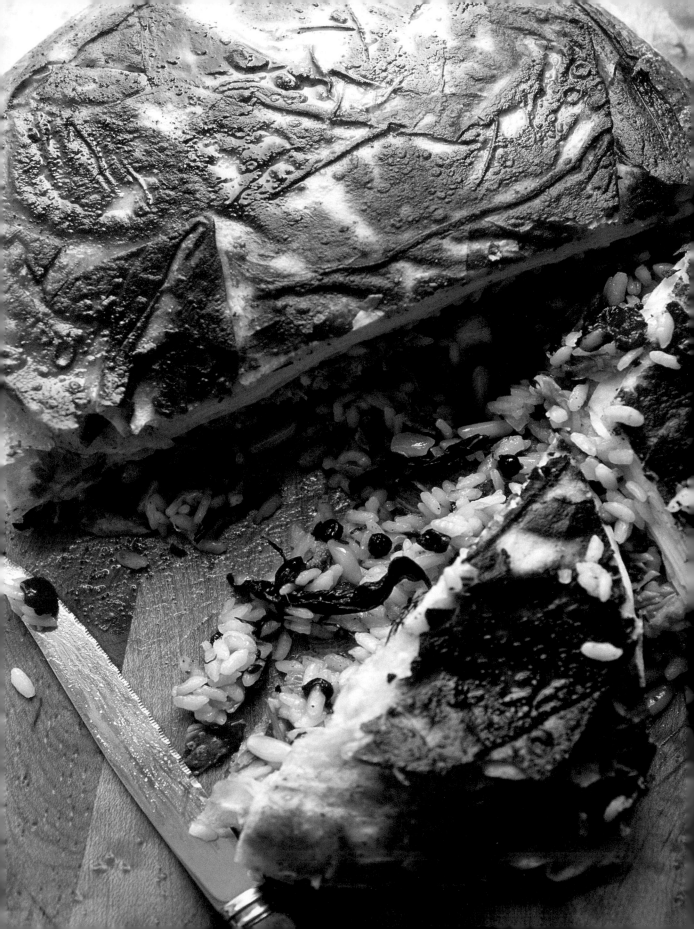

Perdeli Pilaf with Duck Confit, Raisins and Pine Nuts

Perdeli pilaf was a favourite on the Sultan's table. Perdeli means curtain or veiled, so this pilaf is also known as veiled pilaf. Most recipes for perdeli pilaf are made with flaky puff pastry, but my way is to use light and crispy yufka pastry instead. It is almost always prepared in a round shape and cut into wedges when served.

Hidden away in the suburb of Edirnekapı in Istanbul is the Asitane restaurant, renowned for fine Ottoman cuisine based on dishes that were served at a feast given by Sultan Suleiman the Magnificent in 1539. This is a delicious variation on that theme. Confit is any meat slowly cooked in fat and it really is worth using. Duck confit can be bought in tins, or you can make it yourself. Alternatively, use conventionally roasted duck legs.

4	duck legs, confit
2	tablespoons olive oil
4	shallots, finely chopped
2	garlic cloves, crushed
250g	baldo rice or short-grain rice
100g	organic raisins
400ml	chicken stock
100g	pine nuts
1	teaspoon hemp seeds
1	large sheet of yufka pastry, approx. 60 × 60cm, or filo pastry
15g	clarified butter or ghee

Preheat the oven to 180°C fan/gas mark 6.

Remove the meat from the duck legs and shred. Discard the skin and bones.

Heat the olive oil in a large saucepan and sauté the shallots and garlic for 2 minutes. Stir in the rice and raisins, coating thoroughly with the oil. Add the stock and bring to the boil. Reduce to a simmer and cook until the rice is done but still moist. Allow to cool a little, then add the pine nuts and hemp seeds, and combine well.

When working with yufka pastry, just as you would with filo, make sure you keep it under a damp cloth, otherwise it will dry out and break easily. Lay out the yufka sheet, spoon all the pilaf mixture into the centre and scatter the duck meat on top. Fold the yufka edges into the centre to enclose the mixture and make a parcel.

Heat the butter in a large non-stick frying pan and carefully place the yufka parcel directly into the pan. Cook on a low to medium heat for 2–3 minutes until the pastry is golden and crispy. Using a large, flat, slotted spoon, carefully turn it over and cook on the other side for a further 2–3 minutes.

Then place the pan in the oven and cook at 180°C fan/gas mark 6 for 5–6 minutes.

Serve hot.

SERVES 4

Salads

The spring and summer bring to the markets of the Eastern Mediterranean the most wonderful displays of salad ingredients. Fresh tomatoes that have never been anywhere near a hothouse, for example, are an absolute delight, their flavour dancing on the taste buds. The wonderful little gems that are the fruits of the pomegranate, the mouth-watering cucumber, the crunchy nuts and velvety beans, the oranges, the artichokes, the avocados – all in plump abundance. So, for me, there is only one rule when preparing salads: always use the freshest ingredients.

Purslane, Tomato and Avocado Salad

This is a typical salad from the Gaziantep region, where purslane is known as pirpirim. It is often served as an accompaniment to kebabs. Purslane is among the most common greens in spring and summertime in the Eastern Mediterranean. It is known as an edible plant and weed, and its taste is not dissimilar to watercress or spinach. So you can substitute either.

large bunch of fresh purslane, roughly torn

½ **large bunch of fresh flat-leaf parsley, finely chopped**

3 **ripe plum tomatoes, cubed**

1 **avocado, peeled and cut into small cubes**

1 **green pepper, finely chopped**

1 **red onion, cut in thin rings**

juice of ½ **small lemon**

1 **teaspoon pomegranate molasses (see p. 249 for the recipe)**

1 **teaspoon crushed or ground sumac**

2–3 **tablespoons olive oil**

1 **teaspoon paprika**

Combine the purslane, parsley, tomatoes, avocado, green pepper and red onion in a large bowl. In a separate bowl, combine the lemon, pomegranate molasses, sumac, olive oil and paprika. Drizzle over the salad, and season. Serve at once.

SERVES 6

Father's Smoked Aubergine and Hibiscus Salt Salad

The smell of charred aubergines – nutty, smoky and caramelised – is seductive, and that's what makes this salad what it is. Dried hibiscus flowers are used quite a bit in traditional Turkish cuisine and are renowned for their medicinal properties. Here I have made my own hibiscus cured salt, using dried hibiscus flowers. The salt is also delicious with fish.

FOR THE HIBISCUS SALT

- 1 tablespoon dried hibiscus flowers
- 1 tablespoon sea salt crystals

FOR THE SALAD

- 2 medium aubergines
- 3 sweet red peppers
- 1 ripe tomato, finely chopped
- juice of 2 lemons
- 2 tablespoons olive oil
- 3 garlic cloves, crushed
- 1 teaspoon ground cumin
- 50g pack of fresh parsley, chopped
- 3 tablespoons hazelnuts, chopped
- ½ teaspoon hibiscus salt

2 days in advance

Place the dried hibiscus flowers in a food processor and pulse to a rough powder. Place in a small bowl, add the salt, mix well and cover. Allow to infuse for 2 days before using. You'll only need a small quantity for this recipe, but you can keep it in a container for up to a month.

On the day

As with the baba ghanoush recipe (p. 53), place the aubergines directly on to a medium heat source, gas or electric, and keep turning until they are evenly blistered, blackened and soft. This will take 10–15 minutes. Once cooked, place the aubergines in a strong plastic bag and allow to sweat – this will make them easier to peel.

Peel the aubergines and discard the skin. Slice the flesh into very thin strips and place into a large bowl. Any bits of the aubergine that have not cooked should be discarded. Repeat this process for the peppers, also cutting them into thin strips once cooled and peeled.

Gently combine the aubergines and peppers in a bowl with the chopped tomato, lemon juice, olive oil, garlic and cumin, and season to taste.

Sprinkle with the parsley, chopped hazelnuts and ½ teaspoon of hibiscus salt.

SERVES 4

Chicken Liver, Potato and Chilli Salad

2 large potatoes, peeled

4 tablespoons olive oil

400g chicken livers

zest and juice of 1 small lemon

8 spring onions, finely sliced

½ large bunch of fresh parsley, leaves only

1 teaspoon Aleppo chilli (or mild chilli flakes)

2 hard-boiled eggs, sliced

Boil the potatoes until just cooked, then drain and leave to cool. Cut them into cubes.

Meanwhile, heat a tablespoon of oil in a frying pan on a medium heat and sauté the chicken livers until cooked and golden brown. Season, cool, then roughly chop.

Place the diced potatoes, chicken livers, lemon juice and zest, spring onions and parsley in a large bowl and toss gently to combine. Season, drizzle with olive oil and sprinkle with the chilli flakes. Serve with the slices of egg arranged on top.

SERVES 4–6

Smashed Cucumber, Mulberry and Pistachio Salad

I still find it amazing that such a simple dish could be so delicious. It's served at the Ciragan Palace in Istanbul. Mulberries were in season when we were in Turkey shooting the pictures for this book, so I added them and this salad became truly princely! British mulberries are absolutely delicious in season (around July and August), but if you can't get fresh mulberries, use pomegranate seeds or dry berries. Just remember to make a wish upon eating your first mulberry of the season! My great friend Elif assures me it's a must!

4	**small cucumbers, peeled**
100g	**thick plain yoghurt**
40g	**pistachio nuts, lightly toasted**
20	**fresh mint leaves**
4–5	**dill sprigs, chopped roughly**
4	**tablespoons pomegranate molasses (see p. 249 for the recipe)**
6–8	**fresh mulberries**

Place the cucumbers on a large board and, using a rolling pin, smash them into large chunks. Put the broken pieces of cucumber into a large bowl with the yoghurt, pistachios, mint and dill. Gently toss the ingredients to combine, and season.

Spoon into serving plates, drizzle with the pomegranate molasses and top with the fresh mulberries.

SERVES 4

If you wish to grab the sun, first sink deep into the land, my friend, thus does the tree by its roots when reaching for the clouds with fragrant flowers and tasty fruit.

Mahmoud Darwish, Palestinian poet, 1941–2008

Pink Grapefruit, Avocado and Pomegranate Salad with Nasturtium Flowers

2 pink grapefruits

2 large avocados, stones removed, peeled and sliced into thin wedges

½ large bunch of fresh purple basil, leaves only

seeds of 1 large pomegranate

3 tablespoons white wine vinegar

4 tablespoons olive oil

½ teaspoon mild mustard

½ teaspoon pomegranate molasses (see p. 249 for the recipe)

1 teaspoon crushed or ground sumac

6–8 nasturtium flowers

Peel the pink grapefruits, making sure you cut away all the pith, then cut them into individual segments. Place in a large bowl along with any juice, add the avocado, basil and pomegranate seeds, and season. Whisk together the vinegar, olive oil, mustard and pomegranate molasses and pour over the salad. Toss gently to combine, sprinkle with sumac and serve garnished with the nasturtium flowers.

SERVES 4

Tomato, Pomegranate and Sumac Salad with a Pomegranate Dressing

The combination of sumac and tomato was made in heaven. This salad is best in the summertime when you can buy tomatoes that have not been grown in a greenhouse, when they are sweet and delicious. I discovered this salad on my very first trip to Istanbul. It is very common and the simplest of salads, but I was blown away by it!

6 ripe plum tomatoes

seeds of 1 pomegranate

1 teaspoon crushed or ground sumac

½ teaspoon ground cumin

4 tablespoons olive oil

2 tablespoons pomegranate molasses (see p. 249 for the recipe)

Slice the tomatoes and place in a large bowl. Add the pomegranate seeds and combine. Mix together the sumac, cumin, olive oil and molasses in a bowl. Pour over the salad and gently toss. Serve at once.

SERVES 6

Grilled Courgettes with White Cheese and Courgette Flowers

With the courgettes and their lovely and delicious flowers,
I just couldn't resist making this simple yet so yummy salad.

3 **tablespoons olive oil**

3 **courgettes, sliced lengthwise into thin strips**

6 **courgette flowers, trimmed and cleaned**

200g **soft white cheese, such as feta or goat's cheese**

juice of 1 **lemon**

1 **teaspoon nigella seeds**

Heat 1 tablespoon of olive oil in a heavy griddle pan. Grill the courgette strips, roughly 1 minute on each side, until just golden brown. Remove and cool. You may need to do these in batches.

Place the cooked courgette in a large bowl, add the courgette flowers, crumble in the cheese, and season to taste.

Mix the lemon juice, remaining olive oil and nigella seeds in a small bowl. Drizzle over the courgettes, flowers and cheese, toss gently and serve immediately.

SERVES 4

Artichoke, Goat's Cheese and Cherry Salad

juice of 2 **lemons**

8 **baby globe artichokes**

400g **fresh broad beans, unshelled**

100g **fresh peas**

200g **goat's cheese, crumbled**

2 **tablespoons olive oil**

½ **teaspoon ground cumin**

2 **tablespoons pomegranate molasses (see p. 249 for the recipe)**

2 **tablespoons dry cherries**

a handful of **pistachios**

zest of 1 **orange**

Have ready a bowl of water with half the lemon juice in it – save the rest for later. Cut the stalks from the artichokes and remove the outer leaves to reach the tender, light green heart. Then drop the artichoke hearts into the lemon water to avoid discoloration. Bring a small saucepan of water to boil. Add the artichokes, face down, cover and simmer for 15–20 minutes, until the artichokes are tender. Shell the broad beans and add to the pan with the peas in the last 5 minutes of cooking. Remove from the heat and drain, then leave to cool and cut the artichokes into small wedges.

Gently toss the artichokes, beans and peas with the goat's cheese, remaining lemon juice, olive oil, cumin, pomegranate molasses, cherries and pistachios. Sprinkle with the orange zest, and season.

SERVES 4

MEAT

One evening an old farmer went to his well to draw water for his animals; a strange light appeared to come from deep inside, he peered into the darkness, and there, at the bottom, was the moon.

The farmer knew his duty; he must rescue the moon and place it back in the firmament. Finding a rope, he tied a hook to one end and dropped it down into the well where it caught upon a rock. The old man pulled and pulled, strained and puffed, and tugged, eventually the rope broke and he fell on his back.

Staring up into the heavens he saw the moon high in the sky, he cried out in joy, 'Praise be and honour to Allah, I have returned the moon to where it belongs.'

Adapted from *Told in the Coffee House*, stories collected
in Istanbul by Cyrus Adler and Allan Ramsay (1898)

Lamb and Pistachio Kebabs

The best place in the world to eat kebabs is Istanbul, and the Beyti restaurant in Florya, founded more than sixty years ago, is the place to go to try them.

This is a recipe for a typical style of kebab from the Gaziantep region, where pistachios are used widely in all areas of cooking. The secret of this kebab is not to buy ready-minced meat but to either finely chop the meat and mince it yourself or ask your butcher to mince it for you at least twice.

900g	lamb shoulder, minced twice
½	large bunch of fresh parsley, finely chopped
2	red onions, finely grated
2	garlic cloves, crushed
200g	pistachios, chopped
¼	teaspoon ground cardamom
1	teaspoon ground cumin
½	teaspoon paprika
½	teaspoon ground black pepper
¼	teaspoon ground cloves
⅓	teaspoon coriander
pinch of	ground cinnamon
pinch of	ground nutmeg
2	tablespoons olive oil, for brushing

Combine all the ingredients, except for the olive oil. Knead the mixture for at least 10 minutes until smooth and well combined.

Split the mixture into 12 equal amounts, and shape into sausage-like kebabs. Place them in the fridge for 30 minutes.

Brush the kebabs with the olive oil. Heat a griddle (or griddle pan) to a medium heat and cook the kebabs for 12–15 minutes, turning occasionally to cook evenly, until golden brown.

Serve with tomato, pomegranate and sumac salad (see p. 126 for the recipe).

SERVES 6

Sumac and Chilli Spiced Rack of Lamb with Sweet Pomegranate Sauce

FOR THE LAMB

- 3 **tablespoons crushed or ground sumac**
- 1 **teaspoon ground cumin**
- ½ **teaspoon mild chilli flakes or powder**
- 4 **lamb racks, 3 points each, French-trimmed**
- 4 **tablespoons olive oil**

FOR THE SAUCE

- 150ml **pomegranate molasses (see p. 249 for the recipe)**
- 50ml **grenadine**
- 3 **tablespoons honey**
- 50ml **water**

1 hour in advance

Combine the sumac, cumin and chilli in a bowl, and season. Arrange the lamb racks on a roasting tray and rub all over with the sumac mix. Drizzle with olive oil and allow to rest for an hour in the fridge.

Preheat the oven to 200°C fan/gas mark 7.

To make the sauce

Place all the ingredients in a small saucepan, bring to the boil, then reduce to a simmer. Cook for 10–12 minutes, until you have a syrupy consistency and have reduced the liquid by half.

To cook the lamb

Place the lamb racks in the oven and roast for 20 minutes, until golden brown. Remove and rest for 10 minutes. Slice into cutlets and drizzle with the pomegranate sauce.

Serve with baba ghanoush (see p. 53 for the recipe).

SERVES 4

Partridge Dolma

The restaurant at the Ciragan Palace has a reputation for serving food with Ottoman influences. The chefs there create Ottoman dishes for the modern day, and this stuffed partridge dish is no different. It also works well with good-quality chicken.

FOR THE PARTRIDGES

4	**250g partridges**
20g	**butter**
4	**tablespoons olive oil**
6	**small shallots, peeled**
6	**garlic cloves, peeled**
2	**bay leaves**
6	**fresh thyme sprigs**
8	**prunes, stoned and chopped**
4	**dry apricots, chopped**
150ml	**chicken stock**

FOR THE STUFFING

2	**skinless chicken breasts, minced**
6	**dried apricots, finely chopped**
100g	**pistachios, roughly chopped**
10	**thyme sprigs, leaves only, chopped**

Preheat the oven to 180°C fan/gas mark 6.

To prepare the partridges

Bone the partridges or ask your butcher to do this. Lay each bird out flat and skin-down, and season.

To make the stuffing

Combine the stuffing ingredients, and season. Divide the stuffing between the birds, then roll them into a sausage shape to enclose the filling. Using kitchen string, tie securely.

To cook the partridges

Heat the butter and olive oil in a baking tray. Place the partridges in the tray and brown for 3–4 minutes on each side. Add the shallots, garlic, bay leaves, thyme, prunes, apricots and stock. Cover the dish with foil and cook in the oven for 30 minutes. Then remove the foil and cook for a further 8–10 minutes.

To serve

Slice the stuffed partridges, and serve with a few of the shallots, garlic, prunes and apricots. This goes wonderfully with the vermicelli pilaf (see p. 108 for the recipe).

SERVES 4

Baked Kofte

FOR THE KOFTE

- 1 slice of bread, soaked in 100ml milk
- 200g minced beef
- 200g ground pork
- 1 onion, grated
- 1 garlic clove, crushed
- ½ large bunch of fresh parsley, finely chopped
- 1 egg
- ½ teaspoon ground cumin
- ¼ teaspoon red pepper flakes
- ¼ teaspoon paprika
- 3–4 tablespoons plain flour
- 4 tablespoons olive oil

FOR THE SAUCE

- 2 tablespoons olive oil
- 3 large tomatoes, chopped
- 2 tablespoons tomato purée
- 1 teaspoon paprika
- 4 tablespoons fresh oregano leaves

Preheat the oven to 180°C fan/gas mark 6.

To make the kofte

Squeeze the excess milk from the bread and place in a bowl. Add the beef and pork mince, onion, garlic, parsley, egg, cumin, red pepper flakes and paprika. Combine well and season. Split the mixture into 12 equal amounts, shape into balls, flatten slightly, then dust with the flour.

Heat the olive oil in a non-stick pan and cook the kofte for 3 minutes on each side, then transfer them into a small casserole dish.

To make the sauce

Using the same pan that you used to fry the kofte, mix together the olive oil, tomatoes, tomato purée and paprika. Season and cook over a low heat for 5 minutes, stirring all the time. Finally, add the oregano and pour over the meatballs in the casserole dish.

Place in the oven and cook for 20 minutes. Serve hot.

SERVES 4

Honey and Za'atar Glazed Chicken with Salsify and Cauliflower Purée

The salsify season varies, but it is generally available in the spring. Salsify is a light and milky vegetable that is wonderful used in soups and vegetable purées. The leaves are perfect for salads. The roots themselves, which look like dirty wooden sticks, are not the most attractive but they are delicious. You'll need to peel them to reveal the beige-white skin, immediately placing the vegetable in a bowl of water and lemon juice to prevent them from discolouring before cooking.

Salsify, known in Turkey as tekesakall, is very popular in the region and is sometimes known as the oyster plant due to its delicate flavour and very light oyster taste.

This recipe is based on a dish I had in Ankara, and when in season, salsify becomes a key ingredient in pilafs, soups and böreks.

FOR THE CHICKEN

- 1 **large chicken, approx. 1.3kg**
- 4 **tablespoons za'atar (see p. 250 for the recipe)**
- 1 **teaspoon ground cumin**
- 3 **tablespoons fresh root ginger, peeled and grated**
- 5 **tablespoons runny honey**
- 4 **tablespoons melted butter**

FOR THE PURÉE

- 300g **salsify**
- 200g **cauliflower florets**
- 200ml **water**
- 200ml **milk**
- 35g **butter**
- 2 **tablespoons thick double cream**
- 50g **pack of fresh oregano, leaves only, finely chopped**

To cook the chicken

Preheat the oven to 180°C fan/gas mark 6.

Put the chicken on a large roasting tray and season inside and out. Combine the za'atar, cumin, ginger and honey in a bowl, then brush the mixture all over the chicken, drizzle with melted butter, and add a little water to the roasting tray. Place the chicken in the oven and cook for roughly 1 hour 20 minutes, basting it every now and again. When golden in colour and cooked, remove and rest for 20 minutes.

To make the purée

Trim, peel and chop the salsify. Place it in a saucepan with the cauliflower florets, water and milk, and season. Bring to the boil, then reduce to a simmer for 20 minutes. Once soft, drain the salsify and cauliflower, then purée in a food processor with the butter and cream until it is smooth and creamy. Stir in the fresh oregano leaves.

To serve

Carve the chicken and serve with the salsify and cauliflower purée.

SERVES 4

Spice Scented Spring Lamb with Quince and Mustard Relish

FOR THE RELISH

2	**large quinces, peeled, cored and sliced**
100ml	**port**
½	**teaspoon ground cloves**
¼	**teaspoon ground nutmeg**
2	**teaspoons mustard powder**

FOR THE LAMB

¼	**teaspoon ground cinnamon**
¼	**teaspoon ground black pepper**
½	**teaspoon ground cumin**
½	**teaspoon ground cardamom**
¼	**teaspoon ground coriander**
¼	**teaspoon salt**
400g	**lamb tenderloin**
5	**tablespoons olive oil**
800g	**fresh broad beans, unshelled**
15g	**butter**
	handful of fresh mint leaves

To make the relish

Place the quinces in a saucepan with the port, bring to the boil, then reduce the heat and simmer for 35–40 minutes, until the consistency is like jam. Add the cloves, nutmeg and mustard and mix well. Place in a jar ready for when you need to use it.

4 hours in advance

Make a spice rub by combining the cinnamon, pepper, cumin, cardamom, coriander and salt in a bowl. Season the lamb with the spice rub and place in the fridge for around 4 hours.

To cook the lamb

Sauté the lamb in the olive oil over a medium heat for 8 minutes each side, or longer if you like it well done. Reserve any cooking juices. Keep the lamb in a warm place, until ready to serve.

Bring a small saucepan of water to the boil and cook the broad beans for just 3–4 minutes. Drain and cool. Once cooled, remove the skins if you wish.

In another small pan melt the butter and sauté the mint leaves (keep a few aside for garnishing) until just wilted, then add the drained beans and cook for a further 3 minutes. Finally add the meat juices.

To serve

Spoon some broad beans into the centre of each plate. Slice the lamb into 16 pieces, season and arrange on top of the beans. Decorate with mint leaves and serve with the quince relish.

SERVES 4

Pomegranate Glazed Kebabs
with Spiced Pomegranate Chutney

4 garlic cloves, crushed

200ml pomegranate juice

3 tablespoons pomegranate molasses (see p. 249 for the recipe)

4 juniper berries, crushed

10 pink peppercorns, crushed

800g lean lamb fillet, cut into 2.5cm cubes

FOR THE CHUTNEY

seeds from 2 pomegranates

1 orange, peeled and cut into small pieces

2 tablespoons orange juice

4 spring onions, finely sliced

¼ teaspoon cayenne pepper

¼ teaspoon sweet paprika

1 red chilli, de-seeded and finely chopped

3 tablespoons fresh mint, finely chopped

FOR THE GLAZE

4 tablespoons pomegranate molasses (see p. 249 for the recipe)

juice of 1 lemon

1 garlic clove, crushed

1 tablespoon honey

12 skewers

1 day in advance

In a large bowl combine the garlic cloves, pomegranate juice, molasses, juniper berries and pink peppercorns. Add the cubed lamb and mix well. Marinate for at least 2 hours or ideally overnight.

2 hours in advance

Combine all the chutney ingredients in a bowl, season and refrigerate for a couple of hours.

To make the glaze

Combine all the ingredients and keep until you are ready to cook the lamb.

To cook the lamb

Remove the lamb cubes from the marinade, divide evenly between the 12 skewers, and brush with the glaze. Cook the kebabs on a preheated grill, turning frequently and basting with the glaze every now and again as you turn them.

Cook for 10–14 minutes, depending on how pink you like the lamb. Serve immediately with pomegranate chutney.

SERVES 6

Veal Ragù in Aubergines

4	tablespoons olive oil
800g	veal fillet, cut into 2cm cubes
2	onions, finely chopped
2	garlic cloves, crushed
3	ripe tomatoes, cubed
1	long red pepper, seeded and chopped
½	teaspoon paprika
½	teaspoon mild chilli flakes
400ml	veal stock
6	medium aubergines
100ml	vegetable oil
6	large ramekin dishes

Preheat the oven to 200°C fan/gas mark 7.

To make the ragù

Heat the olive oil in a non-stick pan and sauté the veal, onions and garlic for 10 minutes. Season, then stir in the tomatoes, pepper, paprika and chilli flakes. Pour in the veal stock and cook on a low to medium heat for 1 to 1½ hours.

To prepare the aubergines

Cut the aubergines lengthwise into 6 slices. Heat a little oil in a non-stick pan and fry the aubergine slices, a few at a time, adding more oil for each batch, until golden brown on each side. Remove and place on kitchen paper to drain the excess oil.

Line each ramekin dish with 6 aubergine slices, each slice slightly overlapping the preceding one, and hanging over the edge of the dish. Spoon the veal ragù into the centre of each dish and fold over the ends of the aubergine slices to form a lid. Any ragù that you have left can be kept for a garnish.

Cook the ramekins in the oven for 10 minutes.

To serve

Carefully turn each ramekin dish upside down on to the middle of a large serving plate, and drizzle with any of the remaining ragù.

SERVES 6

Poussin with Yoghurt and Tarragon Sauce

Many dishes in Eastern Mediterranean cuisine are cooked with stabilised yoghurt, producing wonderfully light dishes that are very healthy. This was something that I had never done before, but at the Al Halabi, Four Seasons, restaurant in Damascus, cooking with stabilised yoghurt is one of their specialities. So I'm very pleased to be able to adopt this method, one of the oldest in Eastern Mediterranean cooking, for this very contemporary dish.

Use a plain sour yoghurt that is high in acidity (around 4% if you can get it). The yoghurt is stabilised by heating it with egg and cornflour – as directed in the recipe below.

FOR THE POUSSINS

4	poussins, approx. weight 500g each
30g	clarified butter or ghee
½	large bunch of fresh tarragon, finely chopped

FOR THE SAUCE

800g	plain, good-quality sour yoghurt
½	teaspoon ground white pepper
3	garlic cloves, crushed
300ml	chicken stock
1	small egg, beaten
1	tablespoon cornflour
3–4	tablespoons water
½	large bunch of fresh tarragon
5	tablespoons olive oil

To cook the poussins

Preheat the oven to 190°C fan/gas mark 6½.

Place the poussins in a roasting tray, then season and drizzle with the butter. Sprinkle the tarragon over the birds and add ½ a cup of water. Roast for 45 minutes to an hour, basting every now and again, until golden brown and cooked.

To make the sauce

Without putting the pan on the heat, combine the yoghurt, pepper, salt, garlic, chicken stock and egg in a saucepan. Place the cornflour in a bowl and add 3–4 tablespoons of water to make a smooth paste, then add the paste to the yoghurt mixture. Now place the saucepan on a low to medium heat and cook for 12–15 minutes, stirring all the time. Remove from the heat and add the cooking juices from the poussins.

Place half the tarragon in a food processor and process until puréed. Finely chop the rest of the tarragon and combine with the puréed tarragon and 5 tablespoons of olive oil. Then add this to the yoghurt sauce.

To serve

Cut each poussin in half, arrange on a serving plate and spoon over some yoghurt and tarragon sauce. Serve with rice.

SERVES 4

Al Halabi Style Kebabs with Walnuts and Pine Nuts served with Potato Moutabel

Mohamed Hussein of the Al Halabi, Four Seasons, in Damascus is considered to be one of the best chefs in Syria, and that in a country where just about everyone considers themselves to be a good chef! These kebabs, made from a recipe he gave me, are best cooked on a chargrill, but they are also lovely griddled or simply cooked under a hot grill.

FOR THE KEBABS

500g	finely minced lamb, preferably minced twice
1	teaspoon mint
½	teaspoon salt
½	teaspoon ground white pepper
80g	walnuts, roughly chopped
80g	pine nuts, roughly chopped
1	small red pepper, finely chopped
80g	mushrooms, finely chopped
100g	mozzarella, finely chopped

FOR THE MOUTABEL

2	large jacket potatoes, cooked and roughly mashed with their skins
2	tablespoons tahini
2	tablespoons plain yoghurt
3	tablespoons lemon juice
½	teaspoon ground cumin
½	tablespoon hemp seeds
8	long skewers, ideally flat shish skewers

To make the kebabs

Combine all the ingredients in a bowl, then knead for 10 minutes until it resembles a sticky dough.

Shape the kebabs on to the skewers, using roughly 50g for each kebab. Shape the meat around the top end of the skewer, then place in the freezer for 20 minutes.

Remove the kebabs from the freezer and place directly on to a hot chargrill for 6–8 minutes, turning them to cook evenly. Alternatively, cook on a griddle or for longer in a hot oven.

To make the moutabel

Combine the mashed potatoes in a bowl with the tahini, yoghurt, lemon juice and cumin. Season and sprinkle with the hemp seeds.

Serve the kebabs with the potato moutabel.

SERVES 4

Aleppo Chilli Marinated Chicken Kebab

5 tablespoons tomato purée

1 teaspoon mild Aleppo chilli (or you can use mild chilli flakes)

3 tablespoons lemon juice

3 garlic cloves, crushed

½ teaspoon ground white pepper

½ teaspoon salt

3 ice cubes

65ml vegetable oil

4 chicken breasts, cut into 2cm cubes

8 skewers

1 day in advance

In a food processor, combine the tomato purée, chilli, lemon juice, garlic, white pepper, salt and ice cubes. Drizzle in the oil a little at a time as you process, until you get a thick paste. Place the chicken in a bowl and coat well with the paste. Cover and refrigerate overnight.

On the day

To cook, preheat a chargrill or oven grill to high. Scrape the marinade off the chicken (discarding the paste) and arrange the chicken cubes on skewers. Cook for 8–10 minutes, turning to cook evenly on all sides.

Serve with baba ghanoush (see p. 53 for the recipe).

SERVES 4

Jidi Bel Zet – Veal Shank with Saffron and Seven Spice

This dish is normally made with kid – baby goat – and comes from an ancient Damascene recipe. I tried it in a restaurant in the old city. It wasn't actually on the menu, but I went there so many times on various trips that the chef/ owner asked me why I was in Syria so much. When I told him I was there to learn more roughly authentic Syrian cooking, he insisted that I return the next day so he could prepare jidi bel zet in my honour. I couldn't turn down such an invitation, and it was a worthwhile discovery. Here's my interpretation of what he taught me.

4	**veal shanks**
2	**tablespoons plain flour**
8	**tablespoons olive oil**
1	**tablespoon baharat** (see p. 248 for the recipe)
3	**bay leaves**
800ml	**water**
3	**medium sweet potatoes, peeled and cubed**
2	**shallots, finely chopped**
2	**garlic cloves, crushed**
pinch of	**saffron**
juice of ½	**lemon**

Preheat the oven to 160°C fan/gas mark 4.

Dust the veal shanks with the flour. Heat 3 tablespoons of olive oil in a large casserole dish and add the baharat, bay leaves and veal shanks. Sauté for 5–8 minutes, turning the shanks to cook evenly, until golden brown on all sides. Add 800ml of water, cover and transfer to the oven for 1 hour 30 minutes, until the meat is soft and coming away from the bone. Once cooked, remove the veal shanks from the dish with a slotted spoon. Put the stock aside for the sauce.

Meanwhile, heat 3 tablespoons of olive oil in a non-stick pan and sauté the sweet potatoes for 5–6 minutes, until golden in colour. Remove and keep until needed.

Heat the remaining olive oil in a non-stick saucepan and sauté the shallots and garlic for 1–2 minutes. Season and add the saffron and browned sweet potato. Pour in the veal stock and add the veal shanks. Cook for 10 minutes, until the potatoes are soft. Just before serving, add the lemon juice. Serve with saffron rice.

SERVES 4

Yiahni – Slow-cooked Lamb with Spring Onions, Cherries and Lemon

Yiahni, a light Turkish stew, is something very special that my mother makes for me as a special treat when the first of the spring onions are out and the new-season lamb has arrived. It's cooked slowly with plenty of seasonal greens – you can add spinach if you like. The addition of cherries is my touch, giving the dish a sweet and sour flavour. Slow it may be, but this dish is well worth waiting for!

4	tablespoons olive oil
800g	lamb shoulder, cubed
24	spring onions, finely sliced
zest and juice of 2	lemons
300ml	lamb stock
3	tablespoons dry cherries
½	large bunch of fresh parsley, finely chopped
2	tablespoons toasted pine nuts

Heat the olive oil in a large non-stick pan. Brown the lamb for 3–5 minutes, turning to ensure even cooking. Then add the spring onions and cook for a further 5 minutes. Add the lemon juice, zest and stock, then cover and simmer on a low heat for 1½ hours, until the meat is tender. Finally, add the dry cherries and stir in the parsley.

Serve in deep plates, topped with pine nuts and accompanied by a simple pilaf.

SERVES 4

Abu Basti – Lamb, Summer Squash and Tahini

Another ancient dish I discovered in Damascus, which isn't even known to the native Damascenes, was shown to me by Chef Mazin at Safran restaurant. It's a dish that he says has been passed down many maternal generations of his family. Every Syrian family has their own version – here's my summery one.

500g	**leg of lamb, cut into 2cm cubes**
30g	**clarified butter or ghee**
2	**garlic cloves, crushed**
1	**onion, finely chopped**
2	**bay leaves**
750ml	**water**
approx. 1kg	**summer squash, peeled, seeded and cut into 2cm cubes**
3	**tablespoons olive oil**
700ml	**plain yoghurt**
1	**egg yolk**
2–3	**tablespoons tahini**
150g	**baldo or arborio rice**

Preheat the oven to 200°C fan/gas mark 7.

In a large saucepan, sauté the lamb cubes in the butter over a medium heat for 3–4 minutes, until just golden brown. Add the garlic, onion, bay leaves and water. Cover the pan and reduce the heat to low. Cook for 1 to 1½ hours, until the meat is tender. When cooked, remove the meat with a slotted spoon and reserve the stock.

Arrange the squash on a roasting tray, drizzle with olive oil, and season. Roast in the oven until the squash has cooked and turned golden in colour.

In a separate large non-stick saucepan, combine the yoghurt and egg yolk, and season. Add a cupful of the lamb stock and cook for 10–12 minutes over a medium heat, constantly stirring. Add the squash and meat to the cooked yoghurt, and finally stir in the tahini.

Use the remaining stock to cook the rice for 15 minutes, until soft. If you need to, add more water while cooking.

SERVES 4

Potato and Green Chilli Stuffed Kofte in Tomato Sauce

FOR THE STUFFING

- 2 tablespoons olive oil
- 2 potatoes, peeled and finely diced
- 2 green chillies, seeded and finely chopped
- 2 garlic cloves, crushed
- 1 onion, grated
- 50g pack of fresh coriander, finely chopped
- 200g haloumi, finely grated

FOR THE KOFTE

- 500g minced lamb
- 3 tablespoons olive oil, for browning the kofte

FOR THE SAUCE

- 1 tablespoon olive oil
- 1 garlic clove, crushed
- 4 large fresh tomatoes, peeled and puréed
- 1 tablespoon tomato purée
- ½ teaspoon ground cumin

TO SERVE

- 50g pack of fresh coriander, finely chopped
- 50g roughly chopped toasted pine nuts

Preheat the oven to 180°C fan/gas mark 6.

To make the stuffing

Heat the olive oil in a pan and sauté the potatoes, chillies, garlic, onion and coriander for 8–10 minutes, until the potato is cooked. Remove from the heat and allow to cool, then stir in the grated haloumi.

To make the kofte

Season the lamb and place in a food processor. Pulse a few times to get a smooth texture. Take a handful of the lamb mixture and shape into a ball, then make a hole in the middle and fill with a tablespoon of stuffing. Pull the meat over the top and roll to enclose. Repeat with the rest of the meat and stuffing.

Heat 3 tablespoons of olive oil in a non-stick ovenproof pan and brown the kofte on all sides, for 3–5 minutes.

To make the sauce

Heat a tablespoon of olive oil in a non-stick pan. Sauté the garlic for 1 minute, then add the tomatoes, tomato purée and cumin. Cook for a further 5 minutes, then pour the sauce over the kofte, season and place in the oven for 12–15 minutes.

Serve hot, sprinkled with the coriander and pine nuts.

SERVES 4

Kadaifi Schnitzel with Pomegranate Sauce

My new family favourite! I had this on my last trip to Istanbul, at a very modern café. I loved this great idea, as back home I make schnitzel at least once a week. I would love to have been the one to think of it! I prefer to use chicken, but veal or pork works well too. Kadaifi pastry is like a shredded filo pastry, and by pomegranate sauce I mean a simple pomegranate molasses, just a drizzle, nothing more than that.

200g kadaifi pastry

4 tablespoons plain flour, for dusting

2 large eggs, beaten

4 chicken breasts, skin removed

3–4 tablespoons olive oil

20g clarified butter or ghee

6 tablespoons pomegranate molasses (see p. 249 for the recipe)

Allow the kadaifi to dry a little at room temperature for 5–6 minutes, then place in a dish or on a plate and crush slightly using your hands, to get small broken pieces. Place the flour in a separate dish and the eggs in a third dish.

Using a heavy kitchen mallet, beat the chicken breasts as thinly as you can. Heat the oil and butter in a large frying pan. Dip each chicken fillet into the flour, then into the eggs, and finally roll it in the kadaifi pieces. Sauté the chicken for 3–4 minutes on each side on a medium heat, then place on kitchen paper to drain.

Place on a serving plate, drizzle with the pomegranate molasses and serve with white butter bean, feta and za'atar crush (see p. 33 for the recipe).

SERVES 4

Lavender and Honey Glazed Chicken with Pine Nut, Chervil and Honey Sauce

Chervil is the most elegant of herbs. It combines a light anise fragrance with parsley's cleansing freshness. The leaves are delicate and are perfect in sauces or soups. If unavailable, use young parsley.

FOR THE CHICKEN

- 3 tablespoons Madeira
- 1 teaspoon dry lavender flowers
- 5 tablespoons runny honey
- 4 chicken breasts on the bone

FOR THE SAUCE

- 100g pine nuts, lightly toasted
- 2 tablespoons olive oil
- ½ large bunch of fresh chervil, finely chopped
- 2 tablespoons runny honey

An hour in advance

Pour the Madeira into a saucepan, add the lavender flowers and honey, bring to the boil, then reduce to a simmer for 2 minutes. Allow to rest for an hour so that the flavours infuse, then season.

To cook the chicken

Preheat the oven to 190°C fan/gas mark 6½.

Arrange the chicken breasts on a roasting tray and glaze with the prepared honey and lavender mixture. Cook in the oven for 45–50 minutes, until golden brown. Reserve some of the cooking juices for the sauce.

To make the sauce

In a large bowl combine the pine nuts, olive oil, chervil, honey and 3 tablespoons of the cooking juices from the chicken, then season.

Serve the lavender and honey glazed chicken with the pine nut, chervil and honey sauce.

SERVES 4

FISH

Sardines Stuffed with Wild Garlic, Tomatoes and Za'atar

approx. 800g **whole sardines**

juice of 1 **lemon**

4 **tablespoons olive oil**

200g **wild garlic leaves and flowers**

1 **teaspoon za'atar (see p. 250 for the recipe)**

3 **large ripe tomatoes, finely chopped**

½ **large bunch of fresh basil, chopped**

3 **tablespoons breadcrumbs**

Preheat the oven to 180°C fan/gas mark 6.

Clean the sardines, removing the heads, the guts and the bones, or ask your fishmonger to do it. Rub lemon juice all over the fish, inside and out, and season.

Put a tablespoon of the olive oil into a pan and sauté the wild garlic leaves and flowers for 1 minute on a medium heat, stirring until the leaves are just wilted. Place the garlic leaves and flowers in a bowl, and add the za'atar, tomatoes, basil and breadcrumbs, and combine well. Spoon some of the filling into each sardine. Secure with cocktail sticks and arrange on a roasting tray.

Drizzle with the remaining oil and bake in the oven for 12–15 minutes.

SERVES 4

Sea Bream with Currants and Pistachios and a Blood Orange Sauce

This recipe is close to my heart, as when I was growing up we had a walnut tree in the garden of our house in the mountains and it was from that tree, fresh or preserved, that my mother and grandmother would prepare a dish very similar to this one.

FOR THE BREAM

- 4 medium-sized sea bream
- 4 ripe plum tomatoes, finely chopped
- 1 red onion, finely chopped
- 3 garlic cloves, crushed
- 4 tablespoons currants
- 200g shelled pistachios, roughly chopped
- 1 tablespoon za'atar (see p. 250 for the recipe)
- 4 tablespoons olive oil
- 2 ripe plum tomatoes, finely chopped (extra)

FOR THE SAUCE

- zest and juice of 2 blood oranges
- 5 tablespoons olive oil

To cook the bream

Preheat the oven to 180°C fan/gas mark 6.

First of all, prepare the fish. Wash, gut and clean the bream, then season the inside.

Combine the tomatoes, onion, garlic, currants, pistachios and za'atar in a bowl. Fill each fish with the mixture and secure with a cocktail stick. Place the fish on a baking tray, drizzle with the olive oil and sprinkle with the extra tomatoes. Then season and bake in the oven for 40 minutes.

To make the sauce

In a bowl, combine the orange juice and zest with the olive oil, and season. Pour a little over the fish just before serving.

SERVES 4

Sea Bass with Wild Garlic en Papillote Poached in Raki

Raki, with slight variations of spelling, is a common anise apéritif enjoyed across much of the Eastern Mediterranean. It was my father's favourite, and I always found it fascinating to watch it turn from a greenish colour to milky white when water was added.

Mezze and raki go hand in hand, though here it is employed as part of a main course recipe. You can use white wine if you can't get hold of raki or are not too keen on the anise flavour.

4	sea bass fillets, approx. 180g each
4	tablespoons olive oil
4	tablespoons lemon juice
2	ripe plum tomatoes, sliced
12	pearl onions, peeled
4	lemon slices
4	bay leaves
100g	wild garlic leaves and flowers, chopped
2	teaspoons crushed or ground sumac
4	tablespoons raki

Preheat the oven to 200°C fan/gas mark 7.

Place each fish in the middle of a piece of greaseproof baking paper and drizzle with olive oil and lemon juice, then arrange a couple of slices of tomato, 3 whole pearl onions, a slice of lemon, a bay leaf and a helping of wild garlic on top. Sprinkle the fish with sumac and finally drizzle with raki and season to taste. Fold the paper to form a parcel round each fish, taking care not to leave any gaps.

Arrange the parcels on a baking tray and place in the oven for 25 minutes.

Serve hot.

SERVES 4

Courgette Flowers Stuffed with Crab and Prawns

The flowers of the courgette plant are delicate and pale, but unfortunately their season is short – July to August – and you might have to look hard to find them. Placing an order with your greengrocer will probably be your best bet. The smaller flowers can be cooked in a tempura style, but the larger ones, common in Italian cuisine, can be stuffed with cheese and deep-fried. When preparing courgette flowers before stuffing, carefully cut out and discard the stigma and stamens as they can be bitter.

FOR THE COURGETTES

12	**courgette flowers**
200g	**white crabmeat, cooked**
100g	**shelled prawns, chopped**
100g	**ricotta**
3	**tablespoons pecorino, grated**
½	**large bunch of fresh oregano, leaves only, finely chopped**
500ml	**vegetable oil, for frying**
	plain flour, for dusting

FOR THE BATTER

80g	**plain flour**
½	**teaspoon salt**
75ml	**cold water**
3	**ice cubes**

To prepare the courgette flowers

Carefully open the flowers and remove the stigma and stamens.

Combine the crab, prawns, ricotta and pecorino in a bowl, then fold in the oregano. Spoon a small amount of the mixture into each courgette flower and gently twist the petals to seal in the stuffing.

To make the batter

Using a fork, roughly combine the flour, salt, water and ice cubes – a smooth batter is not required.

To cook the courgette flowers

Heat the oil in a saucepan to 190°C.

Dust each stuffed courgette flower with flour, dip them into the batter, then gently drop them into the hot oil. Cook a couple at a time for 2–3 minutes, until golden brown, then remove with a slotted spoon and place on kitchen paper to drain. Repeat with all the courgette flowers.

Serve hot, with a simple green salad.

SERVES 6

Warm King Prawn Salad with Pink Radish and Red Onion

FOR THE SALAD

8	small pink radishes, finely sliced
200g	wild rocket leaves
	a handful of fennel leaves
1	red onion, sliced
2	tablespoons olive oil
12	king prawns, peeled, tail left intact
30g	pine nuts, lightly toasted

FOR THE DRESSING

2	tablespoons olive oil
2	tablespoons orange juice
1	teaspoon za'atar (see p. 250 for the recipe)
2	tablespoons red wine vinegar
	a few sprigs of fresh coriander, finely chopped

To make the salad

Combine the radishes, rocket, fennel and onion in a salad bowl. Heat the olive oil in a heavy pan and sauté the king prawns on a medium heat for 2 minutes on each side, until brown. Season and keep warm.

To make the dressing

Combine all the ingredients, and season.

To serve

Serve the salad on 4 plates and sprinkle with the pine nuts. Top each portion with 3 king prawns and drizzle with the dressing. If you wish to make this a really special summer salad, top with nasturtium flowers and sumac.

SERVES 4

Cod in Pistachio and Za'atar Crumbs

The Narenj restaurant is a converted mill that lies in the heart of Old Damascus and faces the entrance to the Jewish Quarter. It serves wonderfully authentic Damascene cuisine, as well as dishes from all across Syria – from Aleppo, Deirezzor and Daraa. Here they have a glass screen in front of the kitchens so that you can see what is being prepared, and there was my fish! This is the recipe they prepared for me.

100g	plain flour
2	eggs, beaten
3	tablespoons fresh breadcrumbs
80g	ground pistachios
1	tablespoon za'atar (see p. 250 for the recipe)
1	teaspoon nigella seeds
approx. 400g	cod fillet, bones and skin removed
5	tablespoons olive oil

Prepare 3 separate plates: one with the flour; the second with the beaten eggs; the third with the breadcrumbs, ground pistachio, za'atar and nigella seeds combined.

Cut the cod into long thin strips. Heat the oil to a high heat in a non-stick frying pan. Dust the cod in the flour, then coat in the eggs and finally roll in the breadcrumb mixture. Sauté the strips of cod for 1–2 minutes on each side, until golden brown. Remove and serve with salad.

SERVES 4

Mint Lemonade

Nothing to do with fish, but it was here at Narenj that I sipped a refreshing mint lemonade and gazed across the breathtaking city skyline, so for your delectation, here is the recipe:

60g	caster sugar
80ml	water
	ice
500ml	water (extra)
500ml	freshly squeezed lemon juice
½	large bunch of fresh mint, just the leaves, chopped
	a few whole fresh mint leaves

In a small saucepan, combine the sugar and water and bring to the boil, then simmer and stir until the sugar has fully dissolved. Remove from heat and allow the syrup to cool.

In a large blender, half-filled with ice, blend together the cooled syrup, 500ml of water, the lemon juice and mint. Serve garnished with some whole mint leaves.

It is in the excitement of that gallop that you see to finest advantage the colours of the city, if you see little else. The dyers' quarter flashes past in purple, the saddlers' in fawn, and the shoemakers' in crimson, as you dash along the open street. Then, plunging into the sombre shadows of the bazaars, new jewels flame out upon your astonished eyes. For the lofty roof has certain holes in it, through which the sunlight leaks in drops and shafts of brilliance like red-hot lance heads. Here, where it strikes upon the shop-fronts, there is the glorious blaze of piled oranges, there the paler light of lemon reflected from some shopkeeper's silk robe. And the mid-street of the bazaar sparkles with ruby, diamond, emerald, amber and sapphire, as the head-dresses and silken robes of passers-by come for a moment within the line of light.

From Damascus to Palmyra, John Kelman (1908)

Sautéed Monkfish with Rose Petal Salt

This recipe works beautifully with scallops too. It was chef Martin from the Al Halabi, Four Seasons, in Damascus who told me about fish with rose petal salt. I tried it and loved it, so now I keep rose petal salt in my cupboard next to my regular salt.

petals from 1 large red rose (washed)

2 **tablespoons crystal sea salt**

approx. 600g **monkfish fillet**

2 **tablespoons olive oil**

10g **clarified butter or ghee, melted**

At least 1 day in advance

Place the petals and salt on a platter and rub together until the petals are well mashed. The petals will break up and colour the salt crystals. I like a chunky texture so I don't overwork the mixture; and whatever you do, don't be tempted to place it in a blender, as you will end up with a purée. Store in a jar and allow the flavours to infuse.

On the day

Cut the monkfish into 12 chunky pieces. Lightly oil the fish and sauté in a hot pan with the clarified butter for 2–3 minutes per piece, until golden brown. Serve topped with a generous pinch of the rose petal salt sprinkled on top. This dish can be accompanied by a deliciously fluffy rice pilaf and a tomato, pomegranate and sumac salad (see p. 108 and p. 126 for the recipes).

SERVES 4

Red Mullet with Pine Nuts, Currants and Gremolata

Gremolata is a garnish or condiment made from parsley, lemon and garlic. It is added to fish or meat dishes to give a more intense flavour. This dish can be prepared using almost any fish, but it turns out particularly well using rich, meaty fish such as mullet.

FOR THE GREMOLATA BREADCRUMBS

½ **large bunch of fresh parsley, finely chopped**

zest of 1 **lemon**

2 **garlic cloves, crushed**

½ **teaspoon ground black pepper**

60g **fresh breadcrumbs**

FOR THE MULLET

4 **whole red mullets**

2 **tablespoons pine nuts, toasted and finely chopped**

3 **tablespoons currants**

zest of 1 **lemon**

juice of ½ **lemon**

plain flour, for dusting

2 **eggs, beaten**

4–5 **tablespoons olive oil**

To make the gremolata breadcrumbs

Combine all the ingredients and keep to one side until needed.

To cook the mullet

Have the fishmonger descale, butterfly and bone the mullet. Combine the pine nuts, currants, lemon juice and zest, and add 3 tablespoons of the gremolata breadcrumbs. Place a spoonful of the stuffing inside each fish. Put the flour, eggs and remaining gremolata breadcrumbs into 3 separate dishes. Coat each fish with flour, then dip them in the egg, and finally coat with the gremolata breadcrumbs.

Heat the olive oil in a frying pan and cook the mullet for 4 minutes on each side, until golden brown. Turn only once, and take care not to let the stuffing fall out.

Serve with a fresh salad.

SERVES 4

Basil and Kadaifi-wrapped King Prawns with Pine Nut Tarator

Kadaifi is basically a shredded filo pastry. It is one of the most popular pastries eaten in Turkey, Syria and Jordan, and is more commonly used in sweet preparations.

This is a personal favourite of mine. It's a showstopper dish – impressive and contemporary, yet so simple to make. You can use the same recipe for wrapping a variety of vegetables too; peppers, aubergines and asparagus are particularly well suited to this. Kadaifi pastry dries very fast, so work quickly and cover it with a damp cloth when you're not using it.

FOR THE PRAWNS

2	**tablespoons lemon juice**
1	**garlic clove, crushed**
½	**teaspoon ground coriander**
½	**tablespoon Tabasco sauce**
12	**large king prawns, shelled and heads removed**
	vegetable oil, for deep-frying

FOR THE TARATOR

1	**slice of bread, crusts removed**
200g	**pine nuts**
2	**small garlic cloves, crushed**
50g	**pack of fresh parsley, roughly chopped**
juice of 1	**lemon**
5	**tablespoons olive oil**
200g	**kadaifi pastry**
24	**large basil leaves**

2 hours in advance

Combine the lemon juice, garlic, coriander and Tabasco sauce in a bowl, add the prawns and coat well, then cover and leave to marinate for 2 hours.

To make the tarator

Soak the bread in a bowl of water then squeeze out the excess. Place the bread in a food processor with the pine nuts, garlic, parsley and lemon juice. Process to a smooth purée, and slowly drizzle in the olive oil. Season, and refrigerate until needed.

To cook the prawns

Heat the vegetable oil in a deep-fat fryer to 190°C. Cut the kadaifi pastry into 12 strips, each about 10cm wide. Lay out a strip of pastry and arrange 2 basil leaves on top. Place a marinated king prawn on one end and roll the pastry around it. Repeat with the rest of the pastry, basil and prawns. Place the wrapped prawns in the deep-fat fryer and cook for 3–4 minutes, until golden brown. Remove to kitchen paper to drain. Rest for 1 minute, then serve with the pine nut tarator.

SERVES 4

There are many varieties of basil – purple, black, opal, Thai. The best way to store any of these varieties is to keep a bunch in a small glass of water, making sure the leaves are kept dry at all times.

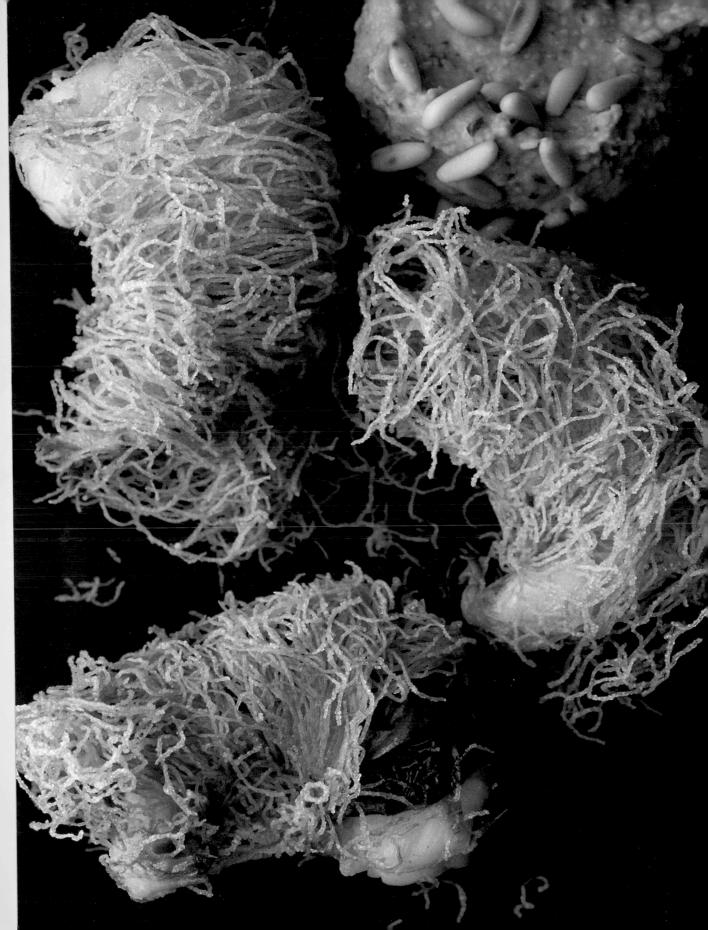

Crispy-coated Whitebait with Quince Aioli

Crispy-coated whitebait is a favourite dish all over Istanbul. Aioli is a Mediterranean type of sauce made with raw eggs, garlic and olive oil. Here I have added a fruity twist using cooked quince to create a tangy aioli, which works really well with the fish. Make sure you use top-quality fresh, free-range eggs for the aioli.

FOR THE AIOLI

- 1 **large quince, grated**
- ½ **teaspoon sugar**
- 1 **garlic clove, crushed**
- 2 **egg yolks**
- 1 **tablespoon lemon juice**
- ½ **teaspoon mustard**
- 100ml **olive oil**

FOR THE WHITEBAIT

- **vegetable oil, for deep-frying**
- 4 **tablespoons plain flour**
- 1 **teaspoon crushed or ground sumac**
- approx. 800g **fresh whitebait**

To make the aioli

Place the grated quince and sugar in a small saucepan and pour in enough water to cover the quince. Bring to the boil, then reduce to a simmer for 3–4 minutes. Strain and cool the quince. Place the garlic, egg yolks, lemon juice and mustard in a food processor. Process and slowly drizzle in the oil. Add most of the cooked quince and fold in, making sure the mixture is well combined. Serve the aioli topped with the rest of the cooked quince.

To cook the whitebait

Heat the vegetable oil in a deep-fat fryer to 190°C. Place the flour and sumac in a bowl, season, and stir to combine. Coat the whitebait with the flour mix, shake off the excess and deep-fry for 2–3 minutes, until golden brown. Serve the whitebait accompanied by the quince aioli.

SERVES 4

Grilled Baby Red Mullet Wrapped in Fresh Vine Leaves with Toasted Citrus and Nasturtium Flower Aioli

Aioli is a classic Mediterranean sauce, made with olive oil, raw egg and garlic. Always make it with top-quality fresh, free-range eggs. This particular aioli is flavoured with fragrant toasted citrus peel and nasturtium flowers. It is the perfect accompaniment to simple grilled fish. Having spotted some baby red mullet on the fish market, I couldn't resist trying this combination.

FOR THE AIOLI

zest of 1	**lemon**
zest of 1	**lime**
zest of 2	**oranges**
2	**egg yolks**
100ml	**olive oil**
50ml	**sunflower oil**
1	**teaspoon mild mustard**
1	**shallot, finely grated**
1	**garlic clove, crushed**
1	**tablespoon lemon juice**
5–7	**orange or yellow nasturtium flowers**

FOR THE MULLET

approx. 800g	**baby red mullet**
40	**vine leaves, fresh or preserved**
3	**tablespoons olive oil**

To make the aioli

Preheat the oven to 90°C fan/gas mark ¼.

Spread the finely grated zest of the citrus fruits on a baking tray lined with greaseproof baking paper and place in the oven for 15 minutes, until lightly toasted. Remove and cool.

Place the egg yolks in a food processor and begin whisking. Slowly drizzle in the olive and sunflower oils until you have a thick and creamy mixture. Season, and combine with the mustard, shallots, garlic, lemon juice and toasted citrus zest. Serve topped with the nasturtium flowers.

To cook the mullet

Clean the baby red mullet, keeping the heads on. Preheat the grill to high. Take one of the fish and wrap it with 2 or 3 vine leaves, then brush the parcel with some olive oil. It's a bit fiddly but ideally you need to completely enclose the fish by rolling the leaves around it and tucking the edges in. Repeat with the rest of the leaves and fish. Place the parcels under the grill and cook for 3–4 minutes on each side.

Serve with the toasted citrus and nasturtium aioli and crusty bread.

SERVES 4

VEGETABLES

The shops abounded with fruit and vegetables. The peaches, nectarines and apricots were excellent; a species of the latter, which they call lousi, possessed the most exquisite and delicious flavour. What we found most agreeable of all was the great abundance of iced water that was exposed for sale in every quarter of the town. It is generally mixed with the fruit of figs or currants, and forms an agreeable and refreshing beverage, in which the Damascenes indulge to profusion.

Of the shopkeepers, I would say in general, that I never saw a more comfortable class of people in their station in life. They are clean, well dressed, of an excellent habit of body, and so extremely civil to strangers, that if they do not have the article which you wish to purchase, they will, unsolicited, walk with you to the place where you can be suited, and not leave until you say, 'This will do: this is good.'

Travels along the Mediterranean, Robert Richardson, MD (1822)

Father's Aubergine Börek

*'Why,' my editor asked, 'is this recipe not in the section with the other böreks?'
The reason is simple: it is not really a börek at all, as it has no pastry, but it
was a dish my father loved making more than any other; it was his börek and
I cannot find it in my heart to change the name. I suppose he called it that
because when the aubergine is cooked with the eggs and flour it makes a kind
of fluffy batter, not so unlike a very light dough. Crispy on the outside and
meltingly mellow on the inside, this dish is a little tricky, but the final result is
very special.*

2	large aubergines
300g	feta
2	eggs, beaten
	large bunch of fresh mint, finely chopped
4–5	tablespoons plain flour
3	eggs (extra)
200g	breadcrumbs
100g	hazelnuts, finely chopped
2	tablespoons olive oil

Cut each aubergine into 12 slices. Place in a colander and sprinkle liberally with salt. Allow them to rest for 20 minutes, then rinse under cold water and dry with kitchen paper.

Meanwhile, make the filling. Mash the feta in a large bowl using a fork. Mix in the eggs and mint, and season.

Lay an aubergine slice on your work surface and spoon on some of the feta mixture, pressing down gently. Top with another slice of aubergine to make a sandwich. Repeat with the remaining aubergine slices and mixture until you have 12 'börek' sandwiches.

Using three dishes, put the flour in one, beat 3 eggs in the second, and combine the breadcrumbs and chopped hazelnuts in the third. Coat each 'börek' in the flour, then coat in egg, and finally give them a good coat of the breadcrumb and hazelnut mixture.

Heat the olive oil in a large non-stick pan over a medium heat. Fry the aubergine sandwiches on both sides for 3–4 minutes, until they're golden brown and crisp. Using a slotted spoon, remove and place them on kitchen paper.

Serve with lemon wedges, and tahini, lemon and sumac sauce (see p. 25 for the recipe).

SERVES 4

Mung Beans with Caramelised Onions and Nigella Seeds

The preparation of this dish could hardly be easier. It is one of the most loved salads on the menu of the Ciragan Palace in Istanbul. If you have never tried mung beans, this is a perfect introduction to these wonderful emerald-green pulses.

250g	dried mung beans, soaked overnight
3	large onions, finely sliced
8	tablespoons olive oil
3	tablespoons red wine vinegar
½	teaspoon mild mustard
½	large bunch of fresh parsley, finely chopped
4	shallots, chopped finely
8	sun-dried tomatoes, finely chopped
1	tablespoon nigella seeds

Drain the mung beans, place in a saucepan and cover with cold water. Bring to the boil then reduce to a simmer and cook the beans for 30 minutes, until they are soft. Remove from the heat, and drain.

Meanwhile, heat half the olive oil in a large saucepan on a low heat and sauté the onions for 20–25 minutes, until they are soft and lightly golden.

Combine the rest of the olive oil, red wine vinegar, mustard, parsley and shallots in a bowl, and season. Add the warm mung beans and toss in the tomatoes. Finally, top with the cooked onions.

Serve hot or cold, sprinkled with nigella seeds.

SERVES 6

Sweet Roasted Peppers on Smoked Aubergine Purée

A smoky, smooth and creamy aubergine purée is a perfect base for sweet roasted red peppers. You can, if you wish, add some grated cheese to the aubergine for a richer taste.

8 long red peppers

3 tablespoons olive oil

2 medium aubergines

juice of 1 lemon

20g butter

80g walnuts, roughly chopped

2 tablespoons thick yoghurt

150g wild rocket

Preheat the oven to 200°C fan/gas mark 7.

Clean the peppers, removing the stems and seeds, and slice lengthwise. Arrange them on a roasting tray and drizzle with the olive oil. Season and roast in the oven for 20–25 minutes.

Place the aubergines directly on a naked gas flame (or on the electric ring if you are using electric) and, taking care, cook on a medium heat for 10–12 minutes, turning occasionally so that the aubergines are chargrilled evenly. The skin will blacken and start blistering and the aubergines will become soft, not to mention that your kitchen will be filled with a wonderful smell. Alternatively bake them in the oven for 10–12 minutes, but the flavour won't be quite the same. Once cooked, place the aubergines in a strong plastic bag and allow to sweat, which will make them easier to peel.

Prepare a bowl of water with some lemon juice and keep it near at hand. Peel the aubergines and discard the skin. Slice the flesh into very thin strips. Any bits of the aubergine that have not cooked should be discarded. Place the peeled aubergines in the lemony water and leave to soak for around 30 minutes. This is what gives the cooked aubergine its characteristic creamy white colour.

Drain the aubergines, discarding the water. Squeeze the slices dry, then mash with a fork and put to one side.

Melt the butter on a medium heat in a non-stick pan and toast the walnuts for 2 minutes. Add the mashed aubergines and cook for a further 2–3 minutes, stirring all the time. Remove from the heat and stir in the yoghurt, and season. Serve the aubergine purée topped with the roasted red peppers and wild rocket leaves.

SERVES 4

Sumac Roasted Tomatoes with Sweet Currants

8 plum tomatoes, halved, or 300g vine cherry tomatoes

1 teaspoon crushed or ground sumac

4 garlic cloves, thinly sliced

4 shallots, finely chopped

large bunch of fresh basil, leaves only

10g brown sugar

½ teaspoon ground cinnamon

50ml olive oil

50g plump currants

Preheat the oven to 150°C fan/gas mark 3½.

Place the tomatoes in a shallow roasting dish. Combine the sumac, garlic, shallots, basil, sugar and cinnamon in a bowl, and season. Scatter this mixture over the tomatoes and drizzle the olive oil over the top. Place in the oven and immediately reduce the heat to 140°C fan/gas mark 3. Roast for 50 minutes.

Remove the roasting tray from the oven and scatter the currants on top, then place back in the oven and roast for a further 20 minutes, until the tomatoes are soft and slightly caramelised.

Serve warm or cold with crusty bread.

SERVES 4

Aubergine Stacks with Pomegranate, Mint and Yoghurt Sauce

This is a stunning-looking dish. Cooking the aubergines so that they are light and crispy is a must, so once they have been fried, drain them on kitchen paper to remove the excess oil. You can substitute pumpkin for the sweet potato if you prefer.

FOR THE SAUCE

200ml	**suzme (strained yoghurt, see instructions on p. 22)**
50g	**pack of fresh mint leaves, finely chopped**
1	**garlic clove, crushed**
1	**pomegranate, seeds and juice**
1	**tablespoon pomegranate molasses (see p. 249 for the recipe)**

FOR THE STACKS

600g	**sweet potato, roughly chopped**
½	**teaspoon salt**
2	**small aubergines**
	plain flour, for dusting
20ml	**olive oil**
10g	**butter**
50g	**pack of fresh mint leaves, finely chopped**
150g	**feta, roughly chopped**

To make the sauce

Combine all the ingredients together and refrigerate until needed.

Preheat the oven to 200°C fan/gas mark 7.

To make the stacks

Place the sweet potato chunks in a saucepan, cover with water and bring to the boil. Add the salt and simmer gently for 15 minutes, until the potatoes are tender. Drain and set to one side.

Cut the aubergines into slices, each roughly 0.5cm thick. Season lightly and dust with flour. Heat the oil in a non-stick frying pan and fry the aubergine slices for 3–4 minutes on a medium heat, until golden on both sides. Place on kitchen paper to drain.

Melt the butter in a saucepan and add the cooked sweet potato, mint and feta. Cook for 1–2 minutes to combine then remove from the heat.

Line a baking tray with greaseproof baking paper and on it alternately layer the aubergine slices and potato mix in 4 neat piles, starting with the largest slices at the bottom and finishing with the smallest slices on top. Place in the oven and bake for 5 minutes.

Serve hot, with the cold pomegranate sauce.

SERVES 4

Go back as far as you will into the vague past, there was always a Damascus. To Damascus years are only moments, decades are only flitting trifles of time. She measures time not by days, months and years, but by the empires she has seen rise and prosper and crumble to ruin. She is a type of immortality. She saw Greece rise, and flourish two thousand years, and die. In her old age she saw Rome built, she saw it overshadow the world with its power; she saw it perish … She has looked upon the dry bones of a thousand empires and will see the tombs of a thousand more before she dies.

The Innocents Abroad, Mark Twain (1869)

Cumin-scented Broth of Celeriac, Summer Squash and Orange

A light and fragrant summery dish, this could be served as either a healthy starter or a main course – a feast for the eyes and the tastebuds! Eastern Mediterranean cuisine boasts a number of similar dishes, all of which burst with the flavour of seasonal produce.

800g	**celeriac, peeled and cubed**
200g	**summer squash, peeled and cubed**
1	**Granny Smith apple, cored, peeled and quartered**
3–4	**celery sticks with leaves, chopped**
juice of 1	**lemon**
1	**orange, halved**
800ml	**vegetable stock**
4	**garlic cloves**
1	**tablespoon honey**
½	**tablespoon cumin seeds, toasted and crushed**
3	**tablespoons olive oil**

Place the celeriac, squash, apple, celery, lemon juice and orange halves in a saucepan with the stock. Bring to the boil, then reduce to a simmer. Now add the peeled whole garlic cloves, honey and cumin, and cook for 30–35 minutes on a low heat, until the celeriac and squash are soft. Finally, add the olive oil, and season to taste. Remove the orange halves and discard.

Serve the broth hot in deep serving plates, topped with a few celery leaves.

SERVES 4

Mahluba Rice with Aubergines, Topped with Feta and Pomegranate Seeds

Mahluba, a preparation of rice baked in the oven, is prepared for the kitchen staff at the Al Halabi, Four Seasons, in Damascus. I think that the guests should feel cheated, for this is not on the restaurant menu.

1	**medium aubergine**
1	**tablespoon vegetable oil**
15g	**clarified butter or ghee**
1	**large onion, finely chopped**
1	**garlic clove, crushed**
4	**tablespoons olive oil**
200g	**short-grain rice**
½	**teaspoon paprika**
500ml	**chicken stock**
200g	**feta, cubed**
seeds from 1	**large pomegranate**

Preheat the oven to 180°C fan/gas mark 6.

Peel the aubergine and slice into 0.5cm thick rounds, then halve each slice to make a half-moon shape. Heat the oil and butter on a medium temperature in an ovenproof dish and fry the aubergine for 3–4 minutes, until golden brown. Remove and place on kitchen paper to drain. Sauté the onion and garlic in the olive oil in the same pan for 1 2 minutes. Add the rice and paprika and stir to coat well, then season. Add the cooked aubergine and pour in the stock. Cover the dish and cook in the oven for 15–18 minutes, until the rice is soft.

Remove and serve hot, topped with chunks of feta and scattered with pomegranate seeds.

SERVES 8

Poached Asparagus with Nasturtium Sauce

Eastern Mediterranean cuisines often make use of flowers and blossoms – they add not only flavour but perfume and colour too. Nasturtiums, the most common of the edible flowers, can be ordered and bought from your greengrocer. They are not overly expensive and are available throughout the year. They look stunning and have a slightly peppery flavour, not dissimilar to watercress. They are delicious in salads and pasta dishes, and also work very well when added to butter, as in this recipe.

100g **fresh nasturtium flowers**
200ml **vegetable stock**
  ice cubes
110g **unsalted butter, melted**
300g **fresh asparagus**
3–5 **fresh nasturtium flowers (extra)**

Remove the stems from the nasturtiums, then place the flowers in a bowl and pour boiling water over them. Leave for 30 seconds, drain and place in a food processor. Add 3 tablespoons of the vegetable stock and pulse until you have a purée. Sit a small bowl over the top of a larger bowl that has been filled with ice cubes. Pour the purée into the smaller bowl. This will preserve the fresh and bright colour of the flowers in the purée. Cool the purée completely, then return it to the food processor. Add the butter and process to combine.

Bring the remaining vegetable stock to the boil, then reduce to a simmer, add the asparagus and cook for 3–4 minutes. Using a slotted spoon, remove the cooked asparagus and arrange in a warm, deep serving plate. Season the asparagus and pour over the nasturtium butter. Garnish with the extra nasturtium flowers and serve.

SERVES 6

Warm Braised Artichokes, Broad Beans and Dill

*Another delicate vegetable dish that is perfect for supper or a light lunch.
Artichokes are loved throughout the Eastern Mediterranean and are frequently
used in everyday cooking.*

2	lemons
4	large globe artichokes
800g	fresh broad beans, unshelled
100ml	olive oil
4	shallots, peeled
900ml	vegetable stock
1	teaspoon sugar
50g	pack of fresh dill, finely chopped
4	tablespoons suzme (strained yoghurt, for directions see p. 22)

Prepare a bowl of cold water with the juice and skin of 1 of the lemons. Cut the stalks from the artichokes and remove the outer leaves to reach the tender, light-green heart. Then drop the artichoke hearts into the lemon water to avoid discoloration.

Shell the broad beans and drop them into a pan of boiling water. Simmer for 3–5 minutes, then drain and cool. Once cooled, remove the outer skins.

Meanwhile, heat the olive oil in a large saucepan and sauté the shallots over a medium heat for 12–15 minutes. Add the broad beans, vegetable stock and sugar, and season. Squeeze the juice from the remaining lemon, add this to the pan and simmer for 10 minutes. Now add the artichokes, cover and simmer for a further 20–30 minutes, until the artichokes are tender. Allow to cool slightly while still in the cooking liquid, then strain.

Serve warm, sprinkled with dill and accompanied by a dollop of suzme.

SERVES 4

SWEETS

Saffron and Pistachio Helva

In the fifteenth century, the palatial Ottoman kitchens were rebuilt to include a structure with six domes called the Helvahane, the House of Helva, where numerous varieties of helva, as well as jams, sherbets and herbal remedies, were made. By the mid-eighteenth century, the six different kinds of helva prepared in the Helvahane were assigned to different chefs, with a hundred apprentices working under each of them. Today, the preparation of helva still marks religious days and occasions such as births and deaths.

Helva is a dessert, a sweet made of semolina, flour, tahini or even vegetables, often enriched with dry fruits and nuts. Helva translates as 'sweetmeat'. My favourite is semolina helva and this recipe here was my father's; you can replace the saffron with vanilla pods as an alternative.

½ teaspoon	saffron threads
2 tablespoons	hot milk
450ml	milk
200g	sugar
90g	unsalted butter
150g	semolina
80g	shelled unsalted pistachios, lightly toasted

Soak the saffron threads in hot milk for 30 minutes.

In a saucepan, warm the milk with the sugar on a medium heat until the sugar dissolves. Keep the mixture warm. In a separate heavy pan, melt the butter. Add the semolina and cook over a low heat, stirring continuously for 20–25 minutes and watching carefully, until the semolina turns a golden brown colour.

Stir the saffron-infused milk into the warm milk and sugar mixture, then add all this to the semolina, stirring vigorously until combined. Turn off the heat, cover and let the helva rest in a warm spot for at least 15 minutes.

Rub off as much skin as you can from the toasted pistachios. Stir them into the helva and serve at room temperature.

SERVES 6

Orange and Hazelnut Cake with Orange Flower Syrup

This is a wheat-free cake, very light and fluffy, soaked in a zesty syrup. Cakes are not as popular as filo pastries in the Eastern Mediterranean, but this is a speciality of the Jewish quarter on the Asian side of Istanbul.

FOR THE SYRUP

150ml	**water**
250g	**caster sugar**
2	**tablespoons orange juice**
zest of 1	**orange**
2	**tablespoons orange flower water**

FOR THE CAKE

5	**eggs, separated**
200g	**caster sugar**
250g	**ground hazelnuts**

TO SERVE

300ml	**thick yoghurt**
2	**tablespoons icing sugar**
4	**passion fruit, seeds and pulp only**

20 x 10cm cake tin

Preheat the oven to 180°C fan/gas mark 6.

To make the syrup

In a saucepan, bring the water to the boil. Add the sugar and orange juice and simmer for 10–12 minutes, until the sugar has dissolved and you have a thick syrupy consistency. Remove from the heat and cool, then stir in the orange zest and orange flower water.

To make the cake

In a bowl, beat the egg yolks with the sugar until you have a pale and creamy mixture. Add the hazelnuts and combine well. In a separate bowl, whisk the egg whites until stiff and glossy, then gently fold them into the hazelnut mixture.

Line and grease the cake tin and pour in the cake mixture. Bake in the oven for 25–30 minutes, until lightly golden. Remove the cake from the oven and evenly pour the cooled orange syrup over the top.

To serve

Combine the yoghurt, icing sugar and passion fruit in a bowl. Serve generously with the warm cake.

SERVES 8–10

Pistachio Revani with Passion Fruit Syrup

This is another recipe that brings back fond memories of my childhood. Revani, a soft semolina cake, is sticky and delicious. This is a modernised version.

FOR THE SYRUP

350g **caster sugar**

10 **passion fruit, pulp only**

300ml **water**

FOR THE REVANI

85g **unsalted butter, softened**

65g **caster sugar**

2 **large eggs, separated**

45g **pistachios, chopped**

30g **plain flour**

½ **teaspoon baking powder**

85g **semolina**

TO SERVE

4 **passion fruit, seeds and pulp only**

150g **mascarpone**

100g **pistachios, chopped**

15 x 15cm cake tin

Preheat the oven to 170°C fan/gas mark 5.

To make the syrup

Combine all the ingredients in a saucepan and bring to the boil on a medium to high heat. Reduce the heat and simmer for 15 minutes, until syrupy and reduced by almost half. Cool and strain through a fine sieve.

To make the revani

Lightly grease the cake tin.

Beat the butter and sugar in a bowl until light and creamy. Add the egg yolks and fold in the pistachios, flour and baking powder. Gradually add the semolina and mix for 1–2 minutes to combine well. Finally, whisk the egg whites until stiff and glossy, and gently fold them into the cake batter. Spoon the batter into the tin and bake in the oven for 20–25 minutes, until just lightly golden on top. Remove from the oven, pour the cooled passion fruit syrup evenly over the top and allow to soak well.

To serve

Combine the passion fruit seeds and pulp and mascarpone in a bowl. Cut the cake into squares and serve warm, with a spoonful of passion fruit mascarpone and with chopped pistachios scattered on top.

SERVES 6–8

Maple Glazed Roasted Figs with Pistachio Praline

FOR THE PRALINE

75g **pistachios, toasted and roughly chopped**

30g **caster sugar**

10g **unsalted butter, softened**

FOR THE FIGS

12 **large figs**

4 **tablespoons butter, melted**

juice of 2 **pomegranates**

1 **tablespoon pomegranate molasses (see p. 249 for the recipe)**

3 **tablespoons maple syrup**

seeds from 10 **cardamom pods, ground**

Preheat the oven to 180°C fan/gas mark 6.

To make the praline

Place the pistachios, sugar and butter in a small bowl and combine. Line a baking tray with greaseproof baking paper and spread the pistachio mixture evenly over the tray. Bake in the oven for 5–6 minutes, then turn off the heat and leave in the oven while the praline cools. Once cooled, remove from the oven and break the praline into small pieces, using a rolling pin.

To cook the figs

Reheat the oven to 180°C fan/gas mark 6.

Trim the figs and cut a cross into the top of each, cutting halfway down into the flesh. Brush with the melted butter and arrange them on a roasting tray.

In a separate bowl, combine the pomegranate juice, pomegranate molasses, maple syrup and cardamom, drizzle over the figs and cook in the oven for 12–15 minutes, until soft and lightly caramelised.

Serve the figs straight from the oven, topped with the pistachio praline.

SERVES 4

Fig and Cardamom Ice Cream

I just adore figs! Gooey and toffee-like, they make this ice cream a very
beautiful dessert indeed, particularly with the added hint of cardamom.
Sometimes I sprinkle on some caramelised pistachios before serving too.
This can be served on its own or to accompany a simple sponge cake.

20	**fresh figs**
165g	**caster sugar**
100ml	**water**
¼	**teaspoon cardamom seeds, ground**
120ml	**double cream**
120ml	**single cream**
3	**tablespoons blood orange juice**

Trim the figs then, using a fork, roughly mash them, including the skins if they're really fresh. Place the mashed figs in a saucepan and add the sugar and water. Cook over a medium heat for 20–30 minutes, stirring from time to time, until you have a thick, jam-like consistency. Add the cardamom, the double and single cream and the blood orange juice.

Using an ice cream machine, churn the ice cream as per your machine's instructions. If you haven't got an ice cream machine, then place the mixture in a plastic container, cover and place in the freezer. You'll need to stir the ice cream every half an hour for at least 2 hours.

SERVES 6

Pink Peppercorn and Cardamom Meringues with Mulberries and White Chocolate

This is one of my all-time favourite recipes. The delicate pink peppercorn meringues are delightfully crisp and spicy, perfect with the tangy berries. Pink peppercorns are very much loved in Turkish cuisine, being both light and fragrant. Mulberries were what I found in season when I was working on this recipe, but you can use whatever fresh berries you have available.

FOR THE MERINGUES

- 4 **egg whites**
- 220g **caster sugar**
- 1 **teaspoon cornflour**
- ½ **teaspoon white wine vinegar**
- 1 **tablespoon pink peppercorns**

TO SERVE

- 100g **white chocolate, chopped**
- 100g **fresh mulberries**
- ¼ **teaspoon ground cardamom**

To make the meringues

Preheat the oven to 140°C fan/gas mark 3.

Whisk the egg whites until they resemble stiff, glossy peaks. Whisk in the sugar, a little at a time, then fold in the cornflour and vinegar. Make 6 large meringues by roughly scooping dollops of the egg white on to a large baking tray lined with greaseproof baking paper. Grind the pink peppercorns with a pestle and mortar. Rub three-quarters of the ground pink peppercorns through a sieve over the top of the individual meringues. Place the tray in the oven and cook for 1 hour without opening the door. When cooked, the meringues should be a pale honey colour. Turn off the oven and let the meringues cool completely before removing them.

To serve

Warm the chopped chocolate in a bowl over a pan of gently simmering water. Stir until all the chocolate has melted, and put to one side. Place a cooled meringue on a dessert plate and drizzle with some melted chocolate. Rub the remaining ground pink peppercorns through a sieve on top of the white chocolate sauce, scatter on some mulberries, and sprinkle on a little cardamom. Serve immediately.

SERVES 4

Orange and Vanilla Crème Caramels

These need to be made 1 day in advance so that there's time to chill and set them in the fridge.

FOR THE CARAMEL

125g	**caster sugar**
75ml	**water**
2	**tablespoons orange flower water**

FOR THE CRÈME

550ml	**double cream**
zest of 2	**oranges**
1	**vanilla pod**
225g	**caster sugar**
2	**whole eggs**
2	**egg yolks**
6	**ramekins**

To make the caramel

Put the sugar, water and orange flower water into a small saucepan over a low-medium heat. Stir well until the sugar has dissolved. Then increase the heat and cook until the sugar turns darker and caramelises. Pour the caramel into 6 ramekins and leave to cool.

To make the crème

Preheat the oven to 150°C fan/gas mark 3½.

Scrape the seeds from the vanilla pod, and combine the pod and seeds with the cream and orange zest in a saucepan over a low heat. Remove from the heat and leave to infuse for around 30 minutes, then remove the vanilla pod.

In a large bowl, whisk the sugar, whole eggs and egg yolks together until thick and creamy. Slowly pour the cooled cream mixture into the whisked eggs and gently fold in. Top the ramekins up with the crème and place on a deep baking tray. Fill the tray with enough boiling water to come two-thirds of the way up the sides of the ramekins and cook in the oven for 1 hour, until almost set. Remove from the oven and leave the crème caramels to cool in the water. Chill overnight to set.

SERVES 6

Künefe with Passion Fruit and Vanilla Syrup

A deliciously crunchy, creamy and sweet confection, made with finely shredded filo pastry baked until crisp and golden, then soaked in syrup. This is a very common sweet throughout the Eastern Mediterranean and Middle East.

This particular recipe was given to me by the head chef of Al Halabi, Four Seasons, in Damascus, but instead of baladi I've used a combination of mozzarella and mascarpone, which works just as well. Traditionally the syrup is simply made with sugar and water, sometimes flavoured with rose water. This passion fruit syrup is a divine alternative!

FOR THE SYRUP

6	passion fruit, pulp only
300g	caster sugar
700ml	water
zest of 1	orange
seeds of 1	vanilla pod

FOR THE KÜNEFE

300g	kadaifi pastry
150g	clarified butter or ghee, melted
300g	mozzarella, cut into small cubes
150ml	mascarpone
100g	chopped pistachios
2	20 × 20cm baking trays

To make the syrup

Pass the passion fruit pulp through a fine sieve. Discard the seeds but keep the juice. In a saucepan, bring the sugar and water to the boil, then simmer on a medium heat until the sugar is dissolved. Cook until the liquid has reduced by about half. Remove from the heat and add the orange zest, passion fruit juice and the vanilla seeds, stirring well to combine. Put to one side to cool.

To make the künefe

Preheat the oven to 180°C fan/gas mark 6.

Using a sharp knife, cut the kadaifi pastry into 1cm square pieces. Place the pieces in a bowl and add 100g of the butter. Mix well to combine. Take half the buttered pastry and press it down into the bottom of a 20 × 20cm baking tray to create a compact base.

Combine the mozzarella and mascarpone in a bowl, and spread the mixture over the compressed kadaifi base. Top with the remaining kadaifi pastry, again pressing down on to the cheese. Drizzle with the remaining butter and cook in the oven for 15 minutes, until golden brown.

Remove the künefe and carefully tip it in to the second tray, so that the upper side is now on the bottom. Place back in the oven for another 15 minutes. Remove from the oven and evenly pour the syrup all over the künefe.

Serve sprinkled with pistachios.

SERVES 4

Rose Petal Ice Cream

225g **caster sugar**

2 **cups of loosely packed rose petals (washed)**

240ml **double cream**

240ml **milk**

5 **egg yolks**

Place the sugar and rose petals in a food processor and pulse to make a purée. Pour the double cream and milk into a saucepan and add the sugar and rose petal purée. Bring to a simmer over a medium heat, stirring until the sugar is dissolved. Remove from the heat.

Whisk the egg yolks and slowly add to the hot cream mixture, whisking all the time. Return the mixture to a medium heat and cook until it is thick enough to coat the back of a wooden spoon, stirring constantly. Pass the mixture through a fine sieve into a bowl and allow to cool.

Using an ice cream machine, churn the ice cream as per your machine's instructions. If you haven't got an ice cream machine, place the mixture in a plastic container, cover and place in the freezer. You'll need to stir the ice cream every half an hour for at least 2 hours.

SERVES 6

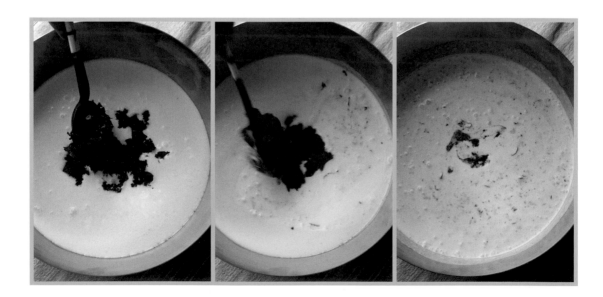

Istanbul Orange and Vanilla Baklava

This, in my opinion, is the undisputed queen of baklava. It is even rare in Istanbul, being prepared only in one or two of the finest eateries. I tasted it for the first time last year in a restaurant in Istanbul and I was just blown away – I'd never had anything like it! The lush creamy and zesty orange layer, sandwiched between the golden crispy filo sheets, veiled in voluptuous and rich sugar syrup, is too amazing to describe. The moment I tasted this stunning dessert, I knew that it would become part of my life and I wanted to be able to prepare it for all those I love, so I asked for the recipe… And I was refused! To refuse to share a recipe is something I have never come across – to me, cooking and eating is about sharing and generosity! Nevertheless, I kept on thinking about that baklava, and went back to try it again, so I could recall the flavours and textures and attempt to recreate it at home.

I failed to come across an 'orange baklava' reference almost anywhere in my research, though I did find something very close. So armed with this and my memories, with some persistence and lots of testing, this recipe was the result. I hope you love it as much as I do!

FOR THE SYRUP

350g **caster sugar**

1 **tablespoon orange juice**

350ml **water**

2 **tablespoons orange flower water**

FOR THE BAKLAVA

2 **large oranges**

seeds of 1 **vanilla pod**

1 **tablespoon orange marmalade**

400g **packet of filo pastry**

150g **butter, melted**

100g **pistachios, roughly chopped**

50ml **mascarpone**

25 × 12cm baking tray

To make the syrup

Place the sugar, orange juice and water in a saucepan and gently bring to the boil. Reduce the heat and simmer for 10–12 minutes, until the syrup becomes thick and glossy. Add the orange flower water and allow to cool.

To make the baklava

Bring a large saucepan of water to the boil and add the whole oranges. Simmer for 45–50 minutes, until the fruit is soft, making sure the oranges are covered by water at all times. Remove the oranges with a slotted spoon and leave to cool. Slice the oranges open and pick out the pips, then transfer all of the cooked orange (including the skin) to a food processor and process to a smooth purée. Place the orange pulp in a muslin bag or cloth and squeeze out as much of the liquid as possible. Discard the liquid and put the orange pulp into a bowl. Add the vanilla seeds and orange marmalade and mix well.

Preheat the oven to 180°C fan/gas mark 6.

Cut the filo pastry sheets to fit whatever size baklava dish you're using. I use a baking tray approx. 25 × 12cm. Keep the pastry covered with a damp cloth while you're not using it. Brush the baking tin with a little butter and start layering the filo sheets, one by one, brushing butter on to each layer. I usually use 8–10 sheets to start with. Do not press the sheets down as you layer them – they should be loosely laid into the tray.

Once you have layered the first half of the filo sheets, evenly spoon over the orange and vanilla purée. Then continue to layer with the rest of the filo sheets as before, another 8–10 sheets on top, each time brushed with butter.

Cut the uncooked baklava into small squares or diamond shapes and place in the oven for 30 minutes. Reduce the temperature to 150°C fan/gas mark 3½ and cook for a further 15–20 minutes, until golden and puffed up. Remove from the oven and, while hot, slowly pour over the cooled syrup, making sure it seeps into every little gap. Sprinkle the pistachios over the top.

Cool completely and serve accompanied by a dollop of mascarpone.

SERVES 10–12

Almond and Apricot Baklava

FOR THE SYRUP

1	vanilla pod
250ml	water
150g	caster sugar
juice of ½	lemon

FOR THE BAKLAVA

200g	unsalted butter, softened
200g	caster sugar
2	eggs, beaten
200g	ground almonds
100ml	melted butter, for brushing
10	sheets of filo pastry
50g	ground almonds (extra)
6–8	apricots, stoned and sliced
150g	pistachios, roughly chopped
100g	runny honey

20 × 10 × 5cm baking tray

To make the syrup

Scrape the seeds from the vanilla pod, and place the pod and seeds in a saucepan along with the water and sugar. Bring to the boil, then reduce to a simmer for 3–5 minutes, until the sugar is completely dissolved. Remove and discard the vanilla pod, add the lemon juice and leave to cool completely.

To make the baklava

Preheat the oven to 180°C fan/gas mark 6.

Place the butter and caster sugar in a mixing bowl and beat to achieve a light and fluffy consistency. Slowly stir in the eggs, and finally fold in the ground almonds.

Brush the bottom of a 20 × 10 × 5cm baking tray with melted butter. Lay in the first sheet of filo pastry and lightly sprinkle with some of the extra ground almonds, then lay on a second sheet of filo, brush with butter and sprinkle with almonds. Repeat until you've used the first 5 sheets. Filo pastry can dry out very quickly, so when you're not using it, cover it with a damp cloth.

On top of the fifth sheet, layer the butter almond mixture and apricots, sprinkle with half the pistachios, and evenly drizzle with honey. Now layer the remaining 5 filo sheets, buttering and sprinkling with the ground almonds as before. Butter the top of the final sheet and sprinkle with the remaining pistachios. Using a sharp knife, cut the baklava into diamond shapes, the size of a generous mouthful.

Bake in the oven for 35–40 minutes, until golden. Remove and, while still hot, pour the cooled syrup over the top, making sure it seeps into every little gap. Allow to rest for a few hours before serving.

SERVES 10

Walnut and Rose Water Baklava

There are more baklava recipes than you can shake a stick at, and in the Eastern Mediterranean almost every family has its own version. Some are made with almonds, others with pistachios. This walnut recipe was my grandmother's and she prepared it every Christmas.

Twelve days before the lavish dinner was served on the evening of the 24th, she would begin, for, so she said, this wonderful confection needed time to mature. The smell of it cooking drove me to distraction. Once cooled, the baklava was soaked in syrup, then covered with a cloth and placed in the larder (which was in fact bigger than the kitchen). No greater torture could have been devised; to know that the baklava was there but not to be allowed to have any was agony. Unable to resist any longer, one morning, before anyone else was out of bed, I sneaked to the larder, carefully opened the door, praying that it would not creak, uncovered the baklava and pulled a little piece from the middle (stupid girl!). Every morning until Christmas I did the same thing. At the end of the meal on Christmas Eve my grandmother brought in the baklava, whipped off the cloth with a flourish, et voilà… Gasps and horrified expressions – the baklava was filled with holes! All eyes turned to me.

FOR THE SYRUP

350g **caster sugar**

350ml **water**

5 **tablespoons rose water**

zest & juice of 2 **lemons**

FOR THE BAKLAVA

400g **clarified butter or ghee, melted**

16 **sheets of filo pastry**

150g **ground walnuts**

500g **new-season walnuts, roughly chopped**

200g **caster sugar**

pink rose petals (washed) to decorate

30 × 20cm **baking tray**

To make the syrup

In a saucepan bring the water and sugar to the boil, then reduce to a simmer and add the rose water. Simmer for 15 minutes, stirring often, so that the sugar dissolves and the syrup thickens. Add the lemon juice and zest, then put to one side to cool.

To make the baklava

Preheat the oven to 180°C fan/gas mark 6.

Brush a large baking tray with a little of the melted butter. Arrange a filo sheet in the bottom of the buttered tray, then brush the top of the pastry with butter and sprinkle with ground walnuts. Cover with another filo sheet, brush with butter and again sprinkle with ground walnuts. Don't press the layers down, and repeat until you've used 8 sheets of filo. Filo pastry can dry out very quickly, so when you're not using it, cover with a damp cloth.

Combine the new-season walnuts and caster sugar and sprinkle half of this on top of the eighth filo sheet. Cover with 8 more sheets of filo, buttering and sprinkling each layer with ground walnuts. The top layer should be buttered and sprinkled with the remaining walnut and sugar mixture. Using a sharp knife, cut the baklava into diamond shapes, the size of a generous mouthful. Spray with water to help crisp up the pastry when cooking and place in the oven for 30–40 minutes.

Remove and, while still hot, pour over the cooled syrup, making sure that you cover all the pastry with the syrup and that it seeps into every little gap. Allow to rest for 48 hours in a dry place.

Serve garnished with a few rose petals and accompanied by Turkish tea.

SERVES 12

Blood Orange and Vanilla Buttermilk Sherbet

Sherbet is a drink originating from Turkey and Persia. To me it is synonymous with sweetness and purity – back home people often say that a child is 'sweet as sherbet'!

1	**vanilla pod**
75ml	**water**
120g	**sugar**
zest of 1	**blood orange**
220ml	**buttermilk**
4	**tablespoons blood orange juice**

Remove the seeds from the vanilla pod, then place the pod and seeds in a saucepan with the water, sugar and orange zest and bring to boil. Remove from the heat and allow to cool a little, then transfer to a bowl and refrigerate until thoroughly chilled.

Once the mixture is cold, remove the vanilla pod and add the buttermilk and orange juice. Churn in an ice cream machine. If you don't have an ice cream machine, place the mixture in a container and freeze, stirring every half an hour for at least 2 hours.

SERVES 4

Yoghurt Panna Cotta with Apricot Mousse

This will need to be prepared a day in advance to allow the panna cotta and mousse to set.

FOR THE PANNA COTTA

3g	**gelatine leaves**
1	**vanilla pod**
200ml	**double cream**
45g	**sugar**
100ml	**plain thick yoghurt**

FOR THE MOUSSE

2–3	**very ripe apricots**
10g	**sugar**
2g	**gelatine leaves**
4	**ramekins or moulds**

To make the panna cotta

Soak the gelatine in a little water to soften. Remove the seeds from the vanilla pod, then place the pod and seeds in a saucepan with the double cream and sugar. On a low temperature, gently heat until the cream comes to the boil. Squeeze any excess water from the softened gelatine. Once boiling, remove the saucepan from the heat and whisk in the softened gelatine until it's dissolved. Pour into a clean bowl and let it cool until it's warm to the touch, then whisk in the yoghurt. Pour the mixture into the ramekins or moulds and leave to set in the fridge for at least 2 hours.

To make the mousse

Stone the apricots, then purée them in a food processor. Place half the apricot purée with the sugar in a saucepan over a medium heat. Meanwhile, soak the gelatine leaves in a little water. Once softened, squeeze out any excess water and remove the gelatine. Stir into the warm apricot purée until it dissolves, then add the rest of the purée. Remove from the heat and transfer to a container to allow to cool, stirring from time to time so that it doesn't set.

Once cooled, pour the mousse on to the semi-set panna cotta, so that you have a thin layer on each portion. Leave the dessert to set in the fridge overnight.

SERVES 4

Pistachio, Rose Water and Honey Ma'amoul Cookies

These ma'amoul cookies are really something else. Use the very best pistachios you can find. Harvested in Iran and Syria, Kabury pistachios are particularly good.

350g	plain flour
165g	clarified butter or ghee
75ml	water
75g	caster sugar
4g	fresh yeast or ½ teaspoon dry active yeast
160g	pistachios, roughly chopped
2	tablespoons runny honey
1	tablespoon rose water
	plain flour, for dusting
20g	whole pistachios

Preheat the oven to 240°C fan/gas mark 9.

Place the flour and butter in a food processor and, using the dough attachment, slowly combine. In a separate bowl, combine the water, sugar and yeast. Add the flour and butter mixture and use your hands to combine all the ingredients. It will feel rather wet and loose, but have faith – this is how it is supposed to be. Place the dough in the fridge for 10 minutes.

Combine the pistachios, honey and rose water in a bowl to produce a sticky mixture. Dust a little flour on to your work surface and divide the chilled cookie dough into 4 parts. Using your hands, roll each quarter into a sausage, roughly 2cm in diameter. With a knife, cut the sausage-shaped dough into discs. Place a small dollop of the pistachio filling into the middle of each disc, pull up the sides of the dough and roll into a ball to enclose the filling. Finally, flatten the cookies back into disc shapes.

Arrange the cookies on a baking tray and place a whole pistachio on top of each one. Bake in the oven for 3–5 minutes. They're ready as soon as they turn golden brown in colour.

MAKES 40–50

Syrian Jewels – Crunchy Sesame and Pistachio Biscuits

Not dissimilar to ma'amoul cookies, these biscuits are a little sweeter. More commonly known as bazarek, these are eaten across Turkey, Syria and Lebanon, and are very popular.

80g	**lightly toasted sesame seeds**
100ml	**thick sugar syrup**
100g	**pistachios, sliced or chopped**
175g	**plain flour**
85g	**clarified butter or ghee**
35ml	**water**
50g	**caster sugar**
2g	**fresh yeast or ¼ teaspoon dry active yeast**
	plain flour, for dusting

Preheat the oven to 180°C fan/gas mark 6.

Place the sesame seeds and sugar syrup in a bowl and mix well, then spread in a thick layer on a tray or flat dish. Spread the pistachios on to a second tray or flat dish.

Place the flour and butter in a food processor and, using the dough attachment, slowly combine. In a separate bowl, combine the water, sugar and yeast. Add the flour and butter mixture and use your hands to combine all the ingredients. It will feel rather wet and loose, but have faith – this is how it is supposed to be. Place the dough in the fridge for 10 minutes.

Dust a little flour on to your work surface and divide the chilled cookie dough into 4 parts. Using your hands, roll each quarter into a sausage, roughly 2cm in diameter. With a knife, cut the sausage-shaped dough into discs, slightly flatten them, then press them first into the sesame and sugar syrup, then into the pistachios. Arrange on a baking tray and bake in the oven for 7–8 minutes, until browned. Remove, cool completely and store in an airtight container (if they last that long!).

MAKES 20

Lemon Balm and Camomile Crème Brûlée

If there is one smell that takes me back to my childhood years, it is the sweet smell of lemon balm. Almost once a week, without fail, our apartment was filled with its smell, as my mother prepared either an almond and lemon balm crème brûlée or made lemon balm cookies.

500ml	**double cream**
3	**sprigs of fresh lemon balm**
8–10	**camomile leaves**
5	**egg yolks**
100g	**caster sugar**
3	**tablespoons demerara sugar**
6	**ramekins**

Preheat the oven to 150°C fan/gas mark 3½.

Put the cream into a small saucepan with the lemon balm and camomile and bring to the boil. Remove from the heat and let the flavours develop for a few minutes. Discard the lemon balm and camomile leaves.

In a separate bowl, whisk together the egg yolks and sugar. Pour the warm cream into the yolks and whisk together to make a custard. Strain the custard through a fine sieve.

Place 6 ramekins on a shallow baking tray. Pour the custard into the ramekins, then pour some boiling water into the shallow tray to create a water bath. Place the tray in the oven and cook for about 20 minutes (it depends on the size of the ramekin or how much custard is in each one). To be sure it's cooked, lightly shake a ramekin – the custard should be set and wobble a little but not appear liquid.

Refrigerate the baked custards for at least 4 hours before serving. Sprinkle some demerara sugar on top, and caramelise by burning with a torch or heating under a hot grill until it's brown and bubbling.

MAKES 6

Pistachio Frangipane Tart

This is something that I love making at home, having been inspired by the wonderful pistachios in Turkish cuisine. The pastry is light, flaky and crisp, and the pistachio frangipane is moist and almost creamy.

125g	**butter, cubed**
50g	**caster sugar**
1	**egg, beaten**
200g	**plain flour**
225g	**butter, cubed**
225g	**caster sugar**
2	**eggs, beaten**
zest of 1	**lemon**
225g	**ground pistachios**
50g	**plain flour**
100g	**cherry jam**
60g	**chopped pistachios**
1	**tablespoon icing sugar, for dusting**
6	**individual tart moulds, 8–10cm diameter**

At least 2 hours in advance

First, make the pastry. Beat the butter and sugar together until light and creamy. Add the egg, then fold in the flour. Combine well until you have a dough. Wrap the dough in clingfilm and chill for 2 hours.

Beat the butter and sugar until light and creamy, then gradually add the eggs and lemon zest. Finally, stir in the ground pistachios and flour and mix well.

Preheat the oven to 180°C fan/gas mark 6.

Roll the chilled pastry to 0.5cm thick and cut 6 rounds 8–10cm across. Use these to line 6 tart moulds, trimming off any excess pastry. Spread the cherry jam on the bases of the tarts and pour in the frangipane mixture. Scatter the chopped pistachios on top and bake in the oven for 25–30 minutes, until the surface is golden. Remove from the oven and cool on a rack.

Dust with icing sugar and serve with a dollop of cream.

SERVES 6

Strawberry and Hibiscus Ice Cream

*Loving hibiscus tea as much as I do, I decided to have a go at making
a strawberry and hibiscus ice cream. It looked and tasted amazing!
It is so easy to make and a very elegant dessert.*

2 **large eggs**

4 **tablespoons caster sugar**

450ml **double cream**

225ml **milk**

1 **tablespoon dried hibiscus
flowers**

300g **strawberries, chopped**

Whisk the eggs in a bowl for roughly 2 minutes, until light and
fluffy. Slowly add the sugar, continually whisking for another
minute. Meanwhile, in a saucepan over a medium heat, bring to
the boil the cream, milk and hibiscus flowers. Once the mixture
has boiled, remove from the heat and allow to infuse for 10–15
minutes. Strain and discard the flowers. Then add the cream and
milk mixture to the eggs and sugar and stir until fully combined.
Finally stir in the strawberries.

Using an ice cream machine, churn the ice cream as per your
machine's instructions. If you haven't got an ice cream machine,
place the mixture in a plastic container, cover and place in the
freezer. You'll need to stir the ice cream every half an hour for at
least 2 hours.

When ready to serve, allow the ice cream to stand at room
temperature for a few minutes to soften first.

SERVES **6**

Rose Petal Jam

400g **young pink rose petals**

400g **caster sugar**

250ml **water**

2 **tablespoons rose water**

juice of 2 **lemons**

6 **200g sterilised glass jam jars with their lids**

2 hours in advance

Wash the petals, making sure that they are clean, de-stemmed and any pollen removed. Place the petals in a bowl and sprinkle with the sugar. Using your fingers, rub the petals with the sugar until you have a soft mass. Leave to infuse for 2 hours.

Place the infused petals in a large saucepan and add the water. Stir and cook on a low heat for 10–15 minutes, until the liquid becomes thick and syrupy. Remove from the heat and stir in the rose water and lemon juice.

Pour the jam into the jam jars. Seal and cool completely.

MAKES 6 × 200G JARS

Some Eastern Mediterranean Store-cupboard Essentials...

Aleppo chilli Mild, sweet, fruity and slightly smoky. You might have to look around for it, but it is available in many Turkish and Middle Eastern foo§d stores, in red and green variations, and you buy it dried. It can be substituted with mild red chilli flakes and a teaspoon of smoked paprika.

Baharat Also known as seven spice, this is a wonderfully warming and aromatic blend of spices that can be added to soups, tomato sauces, lentils and pilafs, and rubbed on fish, poultry and meat. Mix it with a little olive oil and it can be used as a marinade too. It can also be combined with sumac, saffron and turmeric. You can easily make this yourself or buy it ready-made in some supermarkets and Middle Eastern shops. The proportions of the spices used vary depending on who you ask, but here's my version:

> 4 teaspoons sweet paprika
> ½ teaspoon hot paprika
> 4 teaspoons ground cumin
> 4 teaspoons ground black pepper
> 1 teaspoon ground ginger
> ½ teaspoon ground coriander
> 1 teaspoon ground cinnamon

Place the seven spices in a small jar, give it a good shake and there you have it.

Makes 5 tablespoons

Bulgur Finely ground, cracked wheat grains.

Cardamom Known as the 'queen of the spices', cardamom is used in both savoury and sweet cooking. You'll need both pods and ground.

Chickpeas Buy them dried.

Cinnamon (dried)

Coriander (ground)

Cornflour

Cumin (ground)

Cumin seeds

Extra virgin olive oil

Fennel seeds

Ginger (dried)

Hemp seeds

Honey

Lavender (dried)

Marjoram (dried)

Mild chilli (flakes and powder)

Mint (dried)

Mustard (powder and paste)

Nigella seeds These come from a flower that is a member of the buttercup family. They have a sharp, nutty, slightly peppery flavour. Make sure you toast them beforehand to release the flavours.

Orange flower water Also known as orange blossom water. Orange flowers have a citrusy, bittersweet flavour and at the same time warm caramel notes. As well as pastries and sweet dishes, it is also used with chicken, pumpkin, and in pilafs. The secret is to use very little – too much and you will end up with a heavily perfumed dish.

Oregano (dried)

Paprika The true aristocrat of spices, from the noble sweet varieties to the fiercely hot, a spice that I grew up with, that I understand and love.

Parsley (dried)

Peppercorns (black and pink)

Pine nuts

Pistachios Buy them whole, shelled and unsalted.

Pomegranate molasses A thick syrup, made from boiling down pomegranate juice and sugar. It is sweet and sour at the same time. Delicious as a dressing, for marinating meat, or added to slow-cooked stews. Pomegranate molasses is also great to make drinks with.

Fairly readily available, but easy to make at home. Here is a recipe for homemade pomegranate molasses:

1 litre pomegranate juice

115g sugar

4 tablespoons lemon juice

In a large, uncovered saucepan, on a medium heat, stir all the ingredients until the sugar has completely dissolved. Reduce the heat to a simmer and cook for roughly an hour, or until the juice has a syrupy consistency and has reduced to roughly 1 cupful. Pour out into a jar. Allow to cool, then store in the refrigerator for up to 4 weeks.

Rose water

Saffron Can be bought in the form of threads, powder and liquid. Threads are the most expensive; a pinch of saffron is roughly 12 threads.

Sea salt

Sesame seeds Very high in oil content, with a nutty aroma. They're used to make za'atar, tahini and helva.

Sumac You'll see this is a key ingredient for many of my recipes and fortunately it's more widely available now. Any good Middle Eastern food shop will sell it crushed or ground, and even Waitrose stock it now. Sumac is the edible berry from a tree related to the mango. Sumac berries turn from dark pink to purple as they ripen. As they dry and harden, they become the size of peppercorns. Sumac has a fruity aroma and citrusy flavour. Great with fish, salads and in pilafs. Its beautiful purple colour inspired the title of this book!

Suzme (labne) Strained yoghurt (see instructions on p. 22).

Tahini Sesame paste, used widely in Eastern Mediterranean and Middle Eastern cuisines.

Vanilla pods

Walnuts

Yufka Thin sheets of pastry, not dissimilar to filo, used in the cuisines of Turkey, Syria and Greece. If you can't get any, then filo pastry is fine.

Za'atar Both a herb in its own right and a blend of dried herbs. Za'atar the herb has long green leaves and a thyme-like flavour. It is sometimes called wild thyme in English, and it grows along the slopes of the Syrian–Lebanese mountains. The za'atar referred to in this book, however, is the dried herb blend and I've included a recipe below. It's also available ready-made in Middle Eastern shops and some supermarkets.

   2 tablespoons oregano (or thyme)
   1 tablespoon marjoram
   2 tablespoons sesame seeds, lightly toasted
   1 tablespoon sumac
   ½ teaspoon salt

Mix together and store in a jar.
   Try this – drizzle some bread with olive oil, sprinkle with za'atar and eat for breakfast.

Index

Acknowledgements

This work is the result of a long and pleasurable journey, and there are so many people that I would like to thank that it would be impossible to name them all, but in my heart I know them. Let me record my gratitude to the following: Martin Knaubert, at the Four Seasons in Damascus, and his team of chefs, especially head chef Mohamad Helal at the Al Halabi, Aleppo's best-kept secret; Mr Ugur Alparslan, Tuğra restaurant chef, at Ciragan Palace in Istanbul; Musa Dagdeviren, owner of Çiya in Istanbul, and chef Kerem Delibalta; Richard Marston for the elegant book design; the classy and stylish Elif Gönensay in Istanbul, who welcomed us into her home and her heart, thanks for making it real; Felicity Blunt, for taking my hand and leading me to Random House, I am truly grateful; Caroline Gascoigne for making me feel like a real author.

My most special thanks go to Emma Rose for working above and beyond the call of duty, for loving and cherishing this work as much as I do, and to Jonathan (Jonny) Lovekin, without whom there would be no life on these pages…

and to my husband Malcolm, without whom life wouldn't taste the same!